NETSUKES

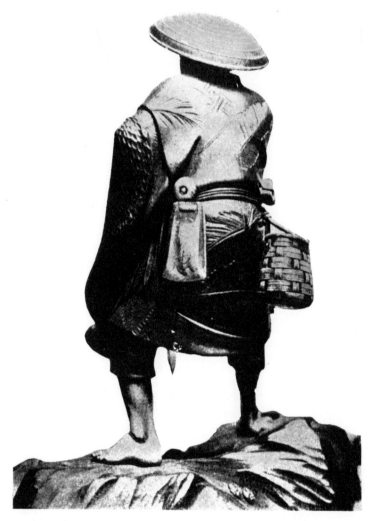

Carved Wooden Figure, showing the way in which Netsukes are used

NETSUKES

BY

ALBERT BROCKHOUS

Translated by M. F. Watty
Edited by E. G. Stillman

ILLUSTRATED

Reprinted by

HACKER ART BOOKS

NEW YORK

1969

First published by Duffield & Co., 1924

Reprinted by

HACKER ART BOOKS, 1969

Library of Congress Catalog Card Number 71-78364

CONTENTS

ILLUSTRATIONS

All the Manjus and Netsukes shown in these illustrations
are reproduced actual size.

PREFACE TO THE ENGLISH EDITION

ALL who are interested in the exquisite Japanese carvings called Netsukes, owe a deep debt of gratitude to Albert Brockhous for having published his masterly treatise on that subject. In order to make this work available to the American collectors who own one or many Netsukes, this English translation has been prepared by Miss M. F. Watty. In this much abridged English version no attempt has been made to reproduce the exquisite colored illustrations or the numerous halftone cuts of the original German edition. The facsimiles of the Japanese signatures have also been omitted, as well as the extensive bibliography. Anyone wishing to study signatures or to delve deeper into the subject should consult the original German work.

E. G. STILLMAN, *Editor.*

PREFACE TO THE GERMAN EDITION

"Everything has its beauty,
But not everyone can see it."

—Confucius.

How is it possible in these days for people with limited means to acquire the original works of a master? Now that there are museums, one might think that it was not worth while for the individual to compete with these institutions, and since collecting became an art and a science, many have abandoned the difficult task of getting together a collection. Now that there has spread among people that desire to make their homes look as luxurious as possible, which has caused the prices of art objects to increase to such an extent that they are unattainable by intellectuals, there is great danger that art as well as handicraft may become a monopoly of the rich.

In spite of this, however, there are still some genuine works of art, really original pieces, which are accessible to him who, through the new and the unusual which ordinarily discourages the masses, is able to distinguish grace and artistic perfection, and who can judge with his own eyes and with a little effort delve into the inexhaustible world of Japanese art, at a time when very few have any appreciation of it.

Whosoever is filled with the desire to understand the art of other peoples, must have sufficient intellectual elasticity to be able to see things with their eyes, and to think and feel as they think and feel. That which in the beginning seemed absurd, will then become logical. In order to enjoy Japanese art, the collector must first endeavor to learn something about the alphabet and the language of the people who have created it.

The domain of Japanese art and Japanese masters is inexhaustible. Painting, plastic art, architecture, and the handicrafts closely related to those fine arts, have, in the course of bygone centuries, produced accomplishments which are only partly equalled by the Japanese today, and which remain wholly unattainable to other people. It is therefore well worth while to collect Japanese things. Fabrics, forged articles and carvings,

earthen wares and lacquer works, paintings and
wood engravings, utensils for religious service,
and ordinary articles of use, are all perfect in
their own way. From the endless number of their
creations, which are well worthy of being studied,
one only needs to pick out one special thing to
discover the ever-increasing joy we derive from
it. To him who possesses knowledge of the subject, every Japanese collection tells of a foreign
people, of an exotic animal and vegetable kingdom, of emperor, nobleman and middle-class, of
church, monks and nuns, of mythological representations which are as adventurous as those of
our own Old Testament or those of our Grecian,
Roman and Germanic mythology; of legends and
stories which at times are exceedingly different
from, and at other times ridiculously similar to,
the Indo-Germanic tales.

The Netsuke, of which this book treats, is a work
of art that can only exist once in this world. It
is found in Japan only, and like the leaves of the
trees, there are never two pieces of it that are
alike. But it is not only the original pieces which
give one pleasure and satisfaction. The Japanese
are such excellent imitators that pieces which are

undoubtedly copies could readily be taken for first-class works of art. Even those which, although marked with a name of the 17th century, have been created some one or two hundred years later are worth owning. It is the object and the artistic execution which attract us, irrespective of whether the work is "genuine" in the sense of art history or not; at any rate it is "genuine" through the spiritualization of material and "genuine" through its technical perfection.

"A thing of beauty is a joy for ever."

The Netsukes deserve more universal consideration than they have been given before the fast moving present generation who still wear them permit them to fall completely into oblivion; and besides, up to this time, hardly anything has been published about them. No complete book on this subject can be written for some time to come, for there are no Europeans who have succeeded in mastering the Japanese and Chinese language and writing, and at the same time are well versed in the mythology, religion, history and legends of the different arts, and above all, of East-Asiatic art. On the other hand, there are no Japanese who have sufficiently studied European art history to understand what we require in the way of historical research.

H. Seymour-Trower wrote around 1890: "A book on Netsukes has yet to be written. The person who can begin and bring to a successful end such a tremendous undertaking, deserves everlasting gratitude." This has yet to be done, but as one who has loved these works of art from the very beginning, I am going for the first time to collect and apply all that has been written on the subject, and to tell what I have observed in so far as I am able. That I am greatly indebted to the authors mentioned in the references quoted goes without saying. Great assistance has been rendered me by the oral explanations of Messrs. Hayashi, Bing and Gonse of Paris, as well as of the Messrs. Okasaki, at that time residing in Leipzig, and to Professor E. Baelz of Tokyo, for his valuable information which enabled me to avoid mistakes that as a layman I would probably have made.

Perhaps I may succeed in interesting, in addition to the small circle of Netsuke collectors, someone who has an artistic inclination for these gems of glyptic art.   Perhaps someone will make use of Pierre Louys' saying in reference to my attempt to write this book: "I am satisfied when, after having read a book, I am able to keep in my memory one sentence that has made me think."

I pursued my Japanese studies as a rest from tiresome work, and spent a great many Sundays writing down what I knew, what I had learned and what I had observed.   Now the printed book lies before me and looks to me as though it demanded more attention.   I regret that I cannot improve upon it nor make it more complete. *"Non pinxisse sed pingere juvat"* seems also to be applicable to me.   If that which I have compiled as a first attempt, shall stimulate comment, and if because of the criticism of my work the desired book on Netsukes should be produced, nobody will be more pleased than

THE AUTHOR.

Leipzig, September 2, 1905.

xvi

PRONUNCIATION—SPELLING

Pronunciation. The vowels of the Japanese language are pronounced as in German; o, u = long o, u. Vowels following one another must be pronounced separately; for instance: Susanoo = Susano-o; u at the end of a word, when preceded by ts and s, and at the end of a syllable, is not pronounced. For instance: Getsu = Gets. Hoku-sai = Hoksai; Netsu-ke = Netske. The consonants are pronounced as in English, ch = tsch, j = dsch; on the other hand y = German j; z = soft s.

Spelling. In the names of the Netsuke carvers there is always a hyphen after the signs in order to clearly show the different parts of the names which consist of several syllables. All other names, and the Japanese and Chinese words remain unseparated.

I have followed the transcription method of Capt. F. Brinkley, Nanjo and Iwasaki, "An unabridged Japanese-English Dictionary" (Tokyo, 1896) for the spelling. A. B.

NETSUKES

NETSUKES

CHAPTER I

USE AND KINDS OF NETSUKES

JAPANESE fashions have in reality remained the same since the eighth century A. D. They are, in principle, the same for men, women and children, and for all classes. As the greatest part of the Netsuke figures represent clothed human forms, it will be well to proceed, first of all, with a minute description of the Japanese dress, which is based upon information received from Professor E. Baelz in Tokyo.

The principal, and very often the only, piece of clothing worn in summer, is a long dressing gown effect, with a skirt, held around the waist by a girdle, to which the name kimono is often applied, and which is usually made of cotton or silk or of hemp-cloth for summer wear. The kimono reaches to the ankles and does not trail when worn outside of the house. The dress, which is called *kaidori* or *uchikake* by women of distinction, and *shikake* by the demi-monde, and which is either embroidered or gaily colored, is worn over the kimono and the obi.

The complete woman's costume in the best taste consists of a hip-cloth, a cotton strip wrapped around the body from the waist down to the knees, and tied around the waist with a belt. Then comes first the undershirt reaching from the shoulders to the hips, or else the long shirt which reaches to the ankles. Then comes the kimono itself, which is in the nature of a shirt, a dress with long pocket-armholes, open in front, buttoned from left to right and tied at the waist with a sash. The kimono would trail on the floor were it not that it is gathered around the hips and held there by means of a belt. In this way, as the left side of the kimono is drawn very much over to the right side, the dress becomes very tight around the legs and this makes a free and easy walk impossible; hence the unbecoming, slow and sliding walk of the well-dressed Japanese woman.

The kimono consists generally of silk of one and the same color, perferably silk crepe; for young girls it is often made of varied colors and in the case of young children, the colors worn are often very bright. Red is not considered suitable for grown-up persons. Over the kimono is worn the overskirt.

The formal costume in winter includes an undershirt, long shirt, and two wadded dresses, made of Habutai silk; their white borders, which cross over the chest, are both visible, and over this comes a kimono of black crepe with the lower border made of colored silk or embroidered.

The dresses embroidered in colors which were so generally worn in Europe by the women, and which were used by the ladies of the houses of the Daimyo and Hatamoto as mantles over their girdles, are not the same as the kimono. They were allowed to trail when worn in the house; on the street, however, they were gathered up. The demi-monde generally wear similar dresses.

The most striking and the most expensive part of a woman's attire is the girdle. It is about four and a half yards long and twelve inches in width, and in some instances made of very heavy gold brocade which is folded lengthwise and then turned over. To tie an obi is a very difficult matter, and it is laughable to see a woman, after she has first made a loop on one side, wind herself in the girdle so to speak.　She turns herself around several times, until the material is practically used up.　Then, with the end that is left and with the help of the loop she made in the first place, and of a soft pad which is inserted, she makes a thing that resembles a pillow or a schoolbag, and which adorns the lower part of the back.

For about one hundred years the girdle ornament was worn in front, especially by women of high rank and by widows as well as by the demimonde, who imitated the aristocratic class in an attempt to attract the men by elegance and refinement rather than by exposing their physical charms.　By girls of the better classes, this ornament is also worn perpendicularly and in this case reaches upward to the neck.

The slit which is formed by the folds of the girdle all the way round, is used to carry pocketbooks, purses, tobacco pouch and pipe.　The little case containing paper which is used instead of a handkerchief, used to be carried in the dress above the girdle.

Both sexes wear stockings with one opening for

the big toe, and, when in the street, sandals made
of straw, or very odd clattering shoes.

The order in which the male clothing is worn
in winter, when there are many layers of clothing,
is as follows: a piece of cloth covering the hips, a
silk or cotton shirt, a wadded under jacket, an
under dress, an over dress and an overcoat.   On
certain festive occasions the men also wear a kind
of silk trousers or rather "divided skirts" and the
Samurai wear a stiff three-cornered over dress on
festal occasions.   The head is mostly uncovered,
but persons belonging to the working class sometimes have their heads protected by an enormous
flat dish-like hat, which is braided out of grass and
split bamboo.   It is held on the head by means of
an inner ring and tied under the chin with straps.
Besides this, large unbrellas made of oilpaper are
used as a protection against the hot sun and the
frequent showers.

The men's kimono is held together with a girdle
four and one half yards long and about six inches
wide.   The obi is the part of the apparel that
interests us most.   To make the men's outfit complete, there must be added, besides the koshisage,
a thing that hangs downward from the hip, a small

pipe with a tobacco pouch, a small medicine box and a portable inkstand. All of these articles are carried in the obi either on the right, the left, or on both sides, as the Japanese fashion neither knows pockets in our sense of the word, nor hooks and eyes, needles, buttons and buttonholes. Lighter objects are put in the deep bulgy hollows of the arms between the obi and the kimono and are prevented from slipping through by means of an ornament: the Netsuke.

The word Ne-tsuke (in Japanese Ne-tske), is composed of ne—root, root-wood, and tsuke—to hang, to attach. The spelling and pronunciation "Netzki," which is used so frequently, is erroneous.

The Netsuke, which remains visible on the upper part of the obi, is tied to a silk string, which passes a few inches farther on through a small button or a slider, ojime, and is tied as closely as possible to the object to which the Netsuke is attached; both are visible below the obi. The ojimes are made of sixty-four different materials and they are put to every practical use and executed in every technique imaginable. The ojime are now being collected and high prices are paid for them. Like the Netsuke,

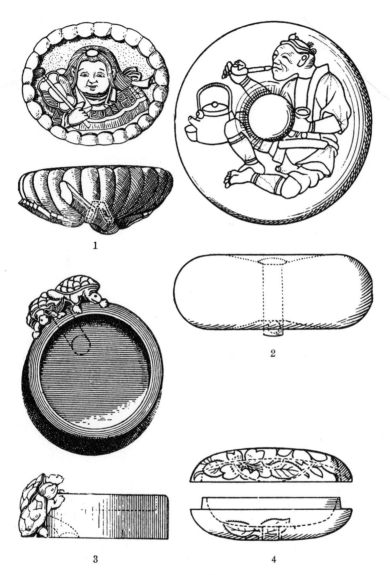

PLATE I

1. Hole Manju, (Ivory). 2. Peg Manju, (Ivory). 3. Ash Container,
(Ivory). 4. Two piece Manju, (Ivory).

they are sometimes marked with the name of the artist.

By its special use, and on account of having one or two holes to pass a string through, the Netsuke is distinguished from all those other products of Japanese art, which are of larger size, and meant for ornaments in the bedrooms, called Okimono. It happens occasionally that these little holes do not appear in the Netsuke figures, when, by a certain position of an arm or a leg, a branch, or a pilgrim staff, small openings are formed through which the silk string may be passed.

The various objects which are worn with the Netsuke are called Koshisage, (hip appendix,) or Sagemono, (hanging object). The medicine box consists of one or more containers made of wood which are usually covered inside and out with varnish in different colors. Often from three to five boxes are put one inside the other and are air tight. Varnished wood is used on account of its lightness and because it does not break easily, and also because it guarantees the most perfect preservation of the restorative which is contained in the box either in the form of pills or powder. These medicine boxes, called Inro, with their

wealth of form and color, are exceedingly charm-
ing and attractive, and therefore the costly favor-
ites of many art collectors. Apparently, the well-
to-do Japanese possessed a large number of Inro
with the accompanying Netsuke, which were worn
as the occasion demanded; simple ones for every
day wear, and finer, more costly and breakable
ones only for special occasions. When not in use,
they were preserved in silk cloth and carefully put
away in drawers.

The writing outfit (Plate XVI, 3) is made either
of wood, ivory, bone, or other material. The long
piece contains, in its hollowed portion, the writing
brush, made of goat, deer, or badger hair, and in
the part that resembles a box, cotton saturated
with China Ink.

The pipe case and the tobacco pouch are usually
made of leather, but sometimes of wood, ivory,
silk (for women), skin, bronze, shell, and other
materials. Their ornamentation as well as that
of the head and mouthpiece of the pipe are of iron
chased and inlaid with bronze, silver, gold and
other kinds of metals. Often-times, instead of the
silk cord, a silver chain is used, and the Ojime then
consists of a silver four-cornered ring, which is

securely attached, and the Netsuke for the most part has the shape of the Manju or button. For many years the Netsuke has in most cases been identical with the pipe case (Plate X, 4). A piece of very hard wood, or bone or horn, longer than the pipe, is decorated or ornamented with figures, and is arranged to contain the pipe. In the latter case, the tobacco pouch is attached in such a manner that it is visible from under the obi, while the pipe case Netsuke holds the tobacco pouch on the upper part of the obi by means of the silk string.

Also the little bag for fire-stone and steel, as well as the tobacco pouch with lighting material and a purse for keys, money, signet and die, were carried in the girdle until the beginning of the 18th century when a kind of wallet or bag came into fashion. But in spite of this new idea, the pilgrim continued and still continues to carry his flask, the entomologist his beetle cage, the fisherman his fish basket, and the Liukiu Islander his dagger (Plate XI, 1) on the girdle by means of a Netsuke. Finally, a small box containing cosmetics is sometimes carried, and by modern people a smelling bottle (Plate XIII, 5) in the form of a small bottle gourd. At times, a single Netsuke serves to attach both the Inro and the purse. Since the beginning of the 16th century, the Netsuke has been the indispensable signet of the Japanese.

Some Netsukes have been found that have no name carved on the underside, and which probably had been made in advance to be kept as stock on hand; and there are many that bear the family names, or the name of the artist who produced the object, or the name of the person who ordered the Netsuke, printed in heavy legible seal writing. Nevertheless, these signet-netsukes are exceptions as compared with the majority of real Netsukes. Also compasses, (Plate VIII, 1) ashcontainers, (Plate I), and flint and steels, (Plate V, 1), are made as Netsukes, so made that they can be used as ornaments with the purse or tobacco implements attached to form a complete set.

A rare art object is the belt-clasp, a Netsuke consisting of a piece of bone, ivory, tortoise shell, or wood in the form of a C. which is used to fasten the purse, both ends of which either appear above and under the sash or are simply slipped on to it.

In view of the fact that the Japanese art productions always have a certain practical purpose, it is not surprising that the Netsukes in many instances are also used as signet, compass, ash container or flint and steel, pipe-case or baskets for miscellaneous articles. Some physicians carried Netsukes which were used to hold medicines, and others to contain a small writing brush. The well-known lacquered Box-Netsukes are containers for all kinds of pleasant, useful or ornamental objects. Brockhous has in his collection a Dutch watch case which measures seven cm. in diameter and which serves the same useful purpose. It is made of pierced gilded bronze, with a plant design border, and on the two surfaces are engraved Dutch landscapes. Its new use is very appropriate in that it is equipped with a Japanese black and brown cover, which bears in embossed silver work the Chinese-Japanese signs representing the name of the owner, a famous wrestler. Instead of using the two holes ordinarily meant for the watch key, the original handle has been placed in the middle of the case.

As the Japanese only learnt to know the pocket-watch for the first time in the 17th century, naturally a Japanese name for it was lacking. The author of the Soken Kisho (1781) describes a

watch to the people of his country as a "Netsuke
which is worn by the Dutch people and is so 'complicated' that the cleverest of Netsuke-carvers cannot imitate it.   Its ticking stops when it is violent-
ly shaken.   Instead you should hold it by you and
play with it and admire its wonderful works.   It
is imported from a Dutch island by the name of
Suzeriya, whose inhabitants are expert astrono-
mers.   The Frenchmen also manufacture these
Netsuke-watches.   Beware of imitations."

From the earliest ages until the present time
two different varieties of Netsukes have been
made: first the flat objects, and then the figures.
These flat Netsukes are called Manju after the
little round cakes, made in the form of a button or
Kagamibuta, and are flat button-shaped and provided with a metal disk.   Only the Netsukes made
in the forms of persons, animals or objects are
described in detail in this book.   Combinations of
both kinds are not rare.   There are turtles with a
removable portion of the shell to which is attached
the string that is then passed down through the
body.   Dragons coiled in circles, and flat-curled
snakes were made whose windings and position
render unnecessary the making of the opening

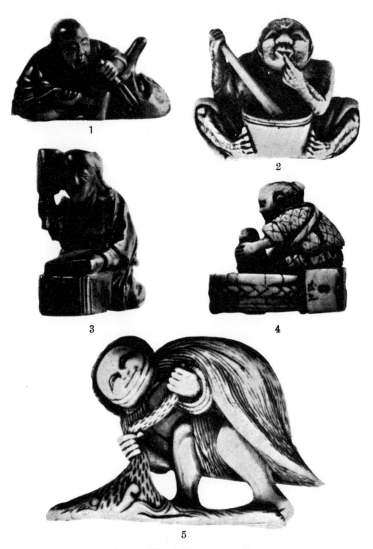

PLATE II—OCCUPATIONS

1. Wood Carver, (wood). 2. Cook, (ivory). 3. Women beating bolt of cloth, (wood). 4. Mother washing baby, (ivory).
5. Fisherman hauling net, (ivory).

through which ordinarily the string is passed, (Plate XIII, 3).

The flat Manjus can be divided into three classes. Those with holes, (Plate I, 1), those with pegs, (Plate I, 2), and those which are formed of two parts (Plate I, 3).

The first class consists of a piece of ivory, wood, horn, or agate, executed in pierced work, bas relief or with sunken relief work on one or both sides.   Either one hole is made in the middle of the button, which unites the upper and lower parts, or two holes are pierced horizontally on the underneath part.

The Manjus belonging to the second class are made of a piece of wood, lacquer, ivory, or metal, through the center of which a loose nail, usually made out of the same material as the Manju, is driven.   The head of the nail prevents it from sliding through the hole.   At the point of this nail, is a hole or a hook for the string.   The top or upper side of these Manjus is decorated with a bas-relief or an etched design.

The Manjus of the third class are composed of two hollow disks with flattened edges, which fit together like a box, and when put together form a button. On the upper part is a hook or eye, in the under part a hole. These are generally finished in gold or red lacquer, wood or ivory, with etched designs, lacquer relief, carving or incrustation.

Many of the Manjus do not bear the name of the artist as they were in many instances manufactured for the trade. Nevertheless, among the second and third class, there are a large number that bear either on the inside or the outside well known names.

Besides these Manjus, there are other Netsukes in the form of buttons. They consist of two parts, a round or sometimes a four cornered piece of ivory with a removable setting in the form of a German Thaler, and made of the same material. They are named after the round Japanese mirror. The setting is of decorated iron, in high or bas relief, intaglio, pierced work, engraving, rusting, chased work, damascened, and in silver, gold, incrusted mother of pearl, polished stone, coral, etc. To the setting is attached an eye to fasten the silk string, while the head piece is provided with a hole underneath to pull the string through.

These are not made by carving masters, but by metal work masters who were accustomed to do work for the classes carrying swords, and who were in the habit of working in similar metals, in the manufacturing of knife handles, sword blades, hilts, etc.

Two more Netsukes of a peculiar kind may be mentioned here, the small chest, for the most part square with rounded corners which can also have the shape of a small ship with a removable cover and which, through the addition of eyes and holes, resemble the Manjus of the third class; and the Ash container Netsuke, (Plate I, 4).

CHAPTER II

THE CARVING OF NETSUKES

THE material used to make Netsukes is much more diversified than can possibly be imagined. The most important consideration, next to the possibility of performing the work with knives and scrapers, is the density of the materials as well as their uniformity.

From the vegetable kingdom are used: various kinds of wood, bamboo, gourds, thick shelled nuts and nutshell. Wood of peculiar forms, even uncut, or parts of famous trees under which, it is said, a hero has rested, pleasant smelling wood like sandal or camphor, wood coated with varnish, lacquer, and amber, peach stones. There are also Netsukes that are made by plaiting the fibre of the Spanish cane or of Wisteria vine.

From the animal kingdom are used: Ivory, walrus tooth, boar and other animal teeth, thigh bones of larger game, deer antlers, buffalo horns from India, and antelope horns, which are used a great deal. Narwhal tusk, which resembles alabaster, is also used and in the middle ages, the Japanese thought this was the horn of the unicorn, a certain remedy against poison and more expensive than gold. But the bones of unedible domestic animals such as fowls, oxen, or horses are not utilized. The domestic pig was, until very recently, unknown. It appears that the art of carving tortoise shell was introduced into Nagasaki from China in the 17th century. Imitation tortoise shell has, since olden times, been produced in absolute perfection from horses hoofs or horn. Even fish bones, mussels, mother of pearl, beaks of toucans etc. are used. Rare but highly valued are the Netsukes made of the skull of cranes. These are used for the Uzume and Shojo figures, the red spots on the side of the skull representing red hair. Some say that the material which was sold by cunning dealers as bones of mermaids appears to have been the lower jaw of the shark.

From the mineral kingdom: Coral, soapstone, nephrite, agate, onyx, rock-crystal, malachite, silver, gold, copper, iron, glass, enameled or varnished clay, multi-colored or painted porcelain, cloisonné, chiseled metal, tin, stained bronze and the peculiar metals named Shibuichi, Shakudo, and Sentoku. These latter, because of their many wonderful rust processes, are especially interesting. The composition of the two first ones, according to Kalischer and Anderson, and of the third, according to Roberts, Austen and Wingham, is as follows:

SHIBUICHI

(Grey Rust)

	Per Cent.
Copper	51.10-67.31
Silver	48.93-32.07
Gold	0.12-trace
Lead	0.25
Iron	a trace
	100.15-99.90

SHAKUDO

(Black Rust)

	Per Cent.
Copper	99.04-94.50
Silver	0.29- 1.55
Gold	0.49- 3.73
Lead	0.11
Iron, Arsenic	a trace
	99.82-99.89

SENTOKU

(pale yellow bronze)

	Per Cent.
Copper	72.32
Zinc	13.10
Tin	8.13
Lead	6.22
Iron, Bismuth, Nickel	0.23
	100.00

Wood is most generally used for Netsukes. The wooden Netsukes were made long before ivory was used and the artistic taste with which they are executed is far superior to that of Netsukes made of ivory. The work is often finer, more suggestive, and warmer. The finely polished old Tsuge-Netsukes, rendered very brown by time, are now considered by the collectors worth their weight in gold, whereas formerly, when Netsukes first became known in Europe, the ivory ones were more valued. "Worth their weight in gold" is to be understood as meaning that the price of a beautiful Netsuke very often brings in gold ten times its weight in wood. Boxwood is used for very expensive pieces. It is extraordinarily hard, yellowish

and has such dense grain, that it almost possesses
the properties of bronze.   This makes it possible
for the carver to attain high perfection in his work.
Mahogany colored sandal wood, which is imported
from China and dyed black, likewise gives wonderful results.   The wood of dates or lotus palms is
also exceedingly hard.   The kernel wood becomes
a dark peach color with age.   This color can also
be artificially produced by burying it in an iron pot
containing earth.

Ebony, which is imported from China, is also
used.   Mi-wa made use of this dense and heavy
ebony, so that the Japanese consider it one of the
proofs of the genuineness of a "Mi-wa" when the
Netsuke sinks in water. But the Japanese are said
to have a way of changing the specific weight of a
Netsuke which cannot be detected.   Other author-
ities state that Mi-wa preferred cherry wood to
box-tree wood.

The carvers also make use of the wood of the
Japanese medlar tree, which is hard and solid;
oak, the timber which is used for the pillars in all
Japanese houses.   The "fire-wood" which is em-
ployed in obtaining fire by friction has a very
agreeable odor and is so perfect that the carvers

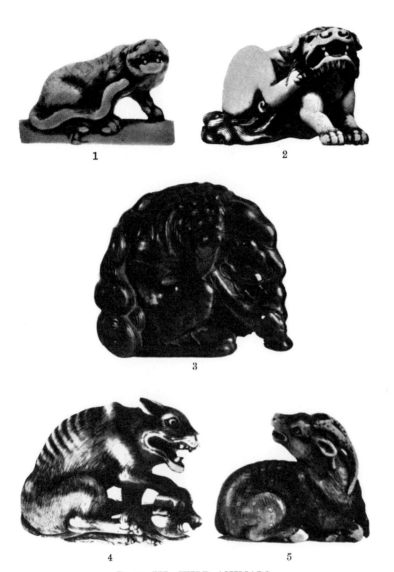

PLATE III—WILD ANIMALS

1. Tiger, (ivory).   2. Lion, (ivory).   3. Elephant, (Lacquered wood).
4. Wild Dog, (ivory).   5. Deer, (ivory).

prefer it to any other kind of wood.   That expensive striped, veined wood of fine hard grain called
Tagaysan is of Chinese origin.

The famous carver Matsu-da Suke-Naga succeeded in putting to good usage the natural spots
of the famous water pines of the province of Hida
without adding color.   The light wood formed the
groundwork for costly lacquer pieces.

Beautiful old wood, which becomes harder as it
gets older, has an unmistakable smooth polish and
a rich color.   This appearance of the wood is of
great importance in distinguishing good antique
from bad modern Netsukes.   The latter, carved of
softer wood, are stained so as to make them appear
old.   The easiest way of proving the genuineness of
a wooden Netsuke is to cut a sliver from the bottom
of one of the Netsuke holes.   If the damage caused
thereby shows clearly through the magnifying
glass, it is certain that the Netsuke is not made out
of heavy, hard and unstained wood.

In former days the wooden Netsukes were
painted several times, then covered with thin varnish, and afterwards, to complete the work, beautifully polished.   Even today, gay-colored Netsukes
are often prepared as in olden times, but these are

of very inferior workmanship and are probably
intended for children's Inros.   In order to give
an old, dirty, dust-covered wooden Netsuke its
original polish, it is sufficient to brush it thoroughly and rub it with a silk cloth.   For cleaning as
well as restoring the lustre and also for the better
preservation of a good old Netsuke, it is well to
cover it with a thin solution of wax or varnish, let
it dry for about two days, then remove the superfluous wax with a piece of feather-quill and brush
the Netsuke with a fine watchmaker's brush until
the original gloss is restored.   If the polish dis-
appears again in the course of time, it only need
be rubbed with silk cloth.   Another way to clean
Netsukes is by rubbing them with a fine piece of
cotton saturated with quick-drying linseed oil and
then polishing with silk.

Next to wood, preference is given by the carver
to fine grained ivory.   As the elephant is not native
to Japan, it has been necessary to import ivory
from China and Korea.   Before the 17th century,
fossil ivory from the Siberian mammoths was
used.   This is especially dense and heavy and as-
sumes an even, soft, light brown tone.   Ivory
Netsukes of a later period, in order to give them

a nicer and antique appearance, are artificially colored. Almost all the ivory imported into Japan during the last century was used for Netsuke carving. Much to the grief of the archæologist, it cannot be denied that a great many old black-brown ivory Buddhas and Saints from distant temples have found their way into the hands of the Netsuke carver, who is willing to pay high prices for the best material.

In more modern times ivory has been used almost exclusively, good and bad, brownish and white. Frequently ivory dust is mixed with a peculiar kind of cement, and pressed into forms copied from famous old Netsukes. Only an expert connoisseur can detect these falsifications.

The outlines of hair, clothes, patterns and other parts, which appear as lines, are blackened with sulphate of iron, or etched with nitric acid, while green coloring is produced by copper vitriol. Vegetable wax is used as covering. Also the good, fine, antique ivory Netsukes are corroded or colored with the juice of berries, the colors running from light yellow to gold yellow. This distinguishes them to good advantage from the cold, milk-white European carvings. Also the color on the front side of the object, which is exposed to sunlight or weather conditions, is fainter than its reverse side.   Some artists, however, used ivory in its natural state.

The cleaning of ivory Netsukes is done with soap and water.   After drying, they are rubbed with a silk cloth and put in the sun, in order to regain the peculiar, transparent milk-like gloss.   The very careful application of a solution of Viennese lime and spirits is recommended, which should be rubbed off after drying with a woolen cloth until the surface becomes bright.

Almost all objects in lacquer are made in the following manner: sixty layers of fine varnish (from Rhus vernix) are put on a surface of hard polished wood, iron, ivory, porcelain, even mother of pearl, tortoise shell, or egg shell.   Each layer is dried in an oven for from twelve to twenty-four hours, hardened and then polished with pulverized charcoal of Magnolia or Lagerstroemia. This proc-ess, on account of the continuous drying and pol-ishing, requires weeks, months and even years to complete the work.   For coloring, the lacquer is mixed with colors such as cinnabar, cochineal, chrome yellow, indigo, or else the colors are mixed with the pulverized camel charcoal which is used for polishing. Gold lacquer is produced from pulverized gold or from the pulverized metal of gold coins, which are composed of ten parts gold and two and six-tenths parts silver. Silver varnish is made out of pulverized silver. Oil is only used for modern lacquer work, as this liquid impairs the durability of the work. Quin mentions two hundred varieties of lacquer. The most important for Netsukes are the following kinds: red varnish; vermilion red varnish; black varnish; several layers of carved varnish, various colors; engraved, gilded varnish; gold dust varnish; gold or silver mosaic; gold bas-relief; gold high-relief; and polished varnish. White and purple lacquer was not used until recently.

It is a fact that the old varnish is so durable and firm that it does not sustain any damage from being left in water for a long time. After a shipwreck in 1873, a wonderful collection of lacquered objects which was being returned to Japan after having been exhibited at the World's Exposition in Vienna, was left at the bottom of the sea for a year and a half. When resalvaged, the old lacquer was found undamaged, while the modern pieces were but a jellied mass.

The first great lacquer artist lived in 1290. It appears that at the end of the 15th century the carving of red and black lacquer was introduced into Japan from China. The carving of layers of lacquer one upon another, in different colors, is accomplished in a most wonderfully skilful manner; carvings of various depths are made which show the different varnish colors, the deepest cuts, which are made in a V shape, showing all the layers separately. Netsukes which consist entirely of lacquer without any wooden foundation, were made much later, and to this present day are executed in a very artistic fashion. Lacquer Netsukes are cleaned with a cotton cloth moistened with linseed oil, which possesses the property of drying quickly, and then polished with paper or silk.

There are also Netsukes in metal, very beautiful ones being made in pure gold and silver, as well as in iron, copper, brass, shakudo, shibuichi, and sentoku. Metal Netsukes can be cleaned like all other articles made of metal, by holding them for five minutes in a receptacle filled with one-quarter of a liter of hot water, in which has been dissolved a very small amount of potash. Then they are rinsed in hot water, until free of all dirt and rust.

One of the most wonderful accomplishments of Japanese art is the use of different materials in one and the same object. On a fungus of wood, for instance, is a snail-shell made of horn, towards which a golden ant is creeping, while an iron beetle is approaching the leaflets of the fungus. Ivory heads and hands on wooden figures are not at all unusual, or eyes made of different color material. So skilfully and easily does the Japanese handle his material, that he even deceives the well trained eye of the art lover. A piece which looks like clay is actually varnish, and that which appears to be wood or bronze may be clay or ivory.

While Europeans are in the habit of working from a model, a copy of which is always before their eyes, the Japanese sculptor works as a rule by free hand without any model. The best Netsuke-carvers were original workers. Other artists by close observation of the object which they have selected for their model, were able to make reproductions from memory. The Japanese artist observes an object until he has memorized the outlines, the dimensions of the parts, and the propor-

tion of the movements, and finally completes the
work by free hand with brush, graving tools,
knives or scrapers.

It seems astonishing, especially to Europeans
who are accustomed to all kinds of drawing para-
phernalia, to see with what assurance the Japanese
artist grasps an outline or a form and reproduces
it by free hand, portraying every motion. He sur-
passes all people of ancient and modern times in
his wonderful ability for reproduction. A bird
flying, a bamboo branch moved by the wind, a horse
rolling itself comfortably, are subjects which are
apparently very simple for him to reproduce. It
can easily be understood that, on account of the
free hand work of the Japanese artist, thousands
and thousands of pieces, neither correspond in
dimensions, nor are slavishly imitated. This is
evidenced by the fact that a few favored subjects
are selected from a large quantity and are used by
different artists. In cases where generations have
passed since the original was made, the artist of a
later period who wishes to make a copy of the
original, does not do so at the cost of his individuality. It is especially interesting to notice how
far he feels himself bound and how he tries to

change the object in order to make it look different from the model.

The Netsuke carver works with fine steel instruments, in long handles, such as borers, chisels and knives, instruments as beautiful as those used for work on gold. Polishing is done by hand. That the polishing of wood did not exist in European art is explained by the fact that the high lustre which is found in the deeper carvings could not be obtained by this process. The roughness which remains after carving is first rubbed with dried horse-tail, then polished with the wet leaves of the aspera tree, and finally cleaned or polished with silk or cotton. Ivory, bone and horn are treated in the same manner, except that pulverized hart's horn, is used to give the articles the desired lustre. Dimmed lustre can be brightened up by applications of wax and hard rubbing with silk. Varnish, pumice stone, and linseed oil are not used.

It would be a great mistake to take it for granted that the Netsuke artist can produce quickly and in large quantities. A Parisian dealer in Japanese wares, Philip Sichel, undertook in 1874 a trip through that country, with the intention of acquiring everything in the way of art objects that was

salable.   He succeeded in getting together an exceedingly interesting collection of over 5000 pieces.

Mr. Sichel relates the following amusing incident: "One day I approached a Japanese who
was seated upon his threshold carving on a nearly
completed Netsuke.   I asked him if he would
sell it to me when it was ready.   The Japanese
laughed and said that it would take me too long
to wait, as he had at least another year and a half's
work before it would be finished.   He showed me
another Netsuke which he carried in his girdle, on
which he had spent several years.   It is true that
he does not work steadily until the work is finished;
on the contrary, he must be in the mood for it.
This is not the case every day, but only when he
has smoked one, two or three pipes and feels refreshed and well satisfied."

It is wonderful to see with what love and devotion and perseverance the Japanese does his work,
and only at such times as he is inspired to work on
the little art object which we possess.   What feel-
ings of joy and sorrow may have moved this sensi-
tive man all that time, and what fate may have befallen him and his family.   What would happen
if the European sculptor only worked on his

masterpiece when he felt refreshed and in good spirits? What if he worked his marble with the greatest concentration instead of being satisfied with doing the modeling in clay and leaving the execution, except for a small amount of finishing work, to his Abbozzatore?

Some people claim that the good Netsukes are no longer imported from Japan to Europe, as they have also begun to collect them in Japan. This fate however the Netsukes share with masks, lacquer works, silk embroidery, silk cloth, porcelains, color prints, embossed works. None of the "trinkets" which were introduced into Europe after the revolution of 1868 have so readily appealed to the public as the Netsukes, none today are as "saleable" as the Netsukes.

One peculiarity of many of the old Netsukes I must mention here, and that is that they resemble pyramids in their form. They have an almost equilateral triangular basis and three almost isosceles sides. A great deal has been written about this characteristic of certain old Netsukes.

After having made a careful study of the subject, Huish made the assertion that undoubtedly in an earlier period it was customary to make the

Netsukes in the shape of trilateral Pyramids, the point of the triangle sometimes placed on top, other times at the bottom. He gives three possible reasons for this: First to prevent the Netsuke from slipping through the girdle; second the natural trilateral form of a figure in a sitting position; third, the natural pyramidal form of the section of an elephant tooth cut in several parts.

According to Brockhous, the three foregoing reasons are less sound than the following: Decidedly there has been for the carver one point of view that stands out above all others, namely that the Netsukes when worn on the girdle should show that side which is the most characteristic. Europeans scarcely ever see the Netsuke in connection with the clothing and figure of the wearer. But if you attach a Netsuke to a silk string and wear it, you immediately find that the artist intended only one side of the Netsuke to show.

In olden times, contrary to the opinion of Huish, and also in the most recent periods, the reverse side of the Netsuke, which rests against the garment, has been cut flatter by the carver, or parts are left to project on both sides in order that the reverse side of the Netsuke may be made to rest close to the body. For the most part the triangular Netsukes are those which do not display nature designs, but imitations of Chinese plastic models. Some of them are in nephrite which already showed the same characteristics of roundness, but which did not present any difficulties in making them triangular. The same thing holds good for Netsukes with a circular intersection, which Huish likewise traces back to the roundness of the elephant tooth. To conclude, it must be mentioned that such triangular Netsukes are also found carved in wood, which material certainly is not put at the disposal of the artist in the form of a section only.

Another characteristic is that almost all the figure Netsukes are made to stand up while they are only intended for hanging. The deeper we go into the study of Japanese art, the more we see that the Japanese never produces anything without a definite purpose. Why does he go through all this trouble? Why does he let himself be influenced in the arrangement of the whole object, in the joining of the under-half, in taking into consideration the center of gravity, the form and the lines? Why are there pieces which apparently carry an over weight, and in spite of it balance on one point only, as for instance a running figure on one toe? Where the equilibrium is taken into consideration, what purpose have those numerous Netsukes which will not stand up?

The possibility of producing a movable ivory worm larger than the hole through which it was inserted into a wooden chestnut is most astonishing, a movable wasp in a wasp's nest, the movable fruit of a lotus tree, a movable head and a movable tongue in the mouth of a ghost and other similar objects of art. Presumably the movable part is made with a slightly wider basis than the opening for which it is intended, and placed in the latter after the wood, through cooking, has become soft. The opening, due to this process, becomes wider and then contracts again as it cools off until it has returned to its original form and size. Or else the movable article is made of a soft adhesive material which becomes hard through drying.

In many cases it would have been very much easier to make the holes for the strings in a more visible place on the Netsuke. In doing it otherwise, one perceives the wise planning, the careful

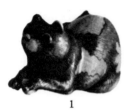

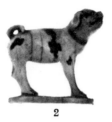

1

2

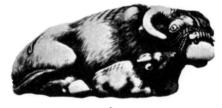

3

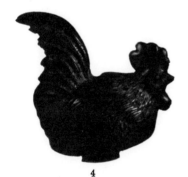

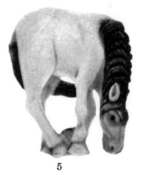

4   5

PLATE IV—DOMESTIC ANIMALS

1. Cat, (ivory). 2. Dog, (ivory). 3. Cow, (ivory). 4. Rooster, (wood).
5. Horse, (ivory).

deliberation exercised by the carver for a thing that may seem to the outsider a mere chance or casual occurrence. The reason of this is, as mentioned before, that the Netsuke has a definite side which is supposed to show.

The holes in the Netsukes often are not of the same size. The larger opening apparently is intended for the knots of the silk string. They are occasionally lined with ivory, or colored horn or edged with stone.

The size of a Netsuke varies considerably, according to its fineness and elegance. The height usually is four cm., but there are some that measure only two cm. in height and others as much as fifteen cm. The width and thickness is mostly two, two and one-half, three and three and one-half cm.

Of the largest and broadest it is said that they were intended for the wrestlers' (Sumotori) use, as these articles correspond to their large and mighty figures.

The age of a Netsuke can in most cases be determined by the wear and tear shown on its surface or holes. There are many modern pieces in soft or hard wood that are very much worn out;

and I have seen many that are old and betray no
signs of wear at all.   As the Japanese greatly
value works of art, even while putting them to
practical use, they handle them with so much care
that an object used for generations does not bear
any traces of having been worn or used.   The
daimyo, the warrior, the samurai, the citizen possesses as many Netsukes as we have cuff buttons
and pendants.   They were most suitable for the
then prevailing style and custom, and the finest
were worn together with the accompanying Inro,
etc., on very special festive occasions only and
therefore retained their new appearance for a
long time.

However, worn Netsukes can always be recognized by the absence of the projecting and sharp
parts which, when worn, had been very much in
the way, and also by the peculiar roundness as well
as by the smooth polish of all the parts.   On the
other hand, the dozens of pieces which were prepared for the European market showed parts that
caught in the folds of the silk kimono.   These
were produced by workmen who manufactured the
same subject continuously, and can be recognized
by the ungraceful carving, if not by the clumsiness

of the form and the poor execution, defects apparent at the very first glance.

The old pieces can also be distinguished from the new by their color. The old wooden and old brown or brown-colored ivory must have that side which is exposed lighter than the side resting against the body.

As Netsukes are very much in demand, the native dealers manufacture all kinds of figures and groups of figures, and by making the two holes in them, they can sell them as Netsukes to the exporter and the layman.

A beautiful genuine Netsuke is not enjoyed with the eyes only; it must be handled in order that the charm of its lilliputian perfectness of form may have its effect upon us. Its polish enables us to follow, with closed eyes, the forms with the fingertips, and so enjoy with all of our senses that which the artist has created in the most surprisingly delicate manner in this creation of boundless detail.

It is true that Japanese art is seldom "monumental" or "grandiose." But it is great in its wonderful perception of the most minute details. Japanese art therefore is very highly praised, perhaps undeservedly highly; it has been sharply abused—much too sharply.   The reproach that it is a short-sighted art, an art by short-sighted for short-sighted people, must sound absurd in the face of the richness and beauty of form which is displayed.   Then too, size is no measure of beauty. If that were the case, then all the beautiful things in this world which the eye can perceive only through the microscope would be unattractive, for instance, a multicolored butterfly scale, or the soft, delicate lines of a diatom.

CHAPTER III

In 1614, the Shogun Kidetada delivered an edict directed against the Christians, that every household must contain a Buddhist idol. From that time, the obedient population gave a great deal more work to the carvers of religious figures, thereby materially aiding a profane plastic art. Not only were the Buddhist Trinity, the four Gods defending the world against the demons, the Temple Guard, and the Buddhist saints and hermits made by thousands, but also life-size portrait statues of priests and heroes. The four supernatural animals also: the dragon, tiger, tortoise and phoenix were executed in bronze, wood and ivory. Although the phoenix often appears in embroidery, Brockhous never saw one in the form of a Netsuke. In the very oldest times, only Chinese-Indian saints and mythological animals were depicted in Netsukes. Later there were added Chinese historical figures, Chinese-Japan-

41

ese gods of fortune, Shoki the devil outcaster and quadruped animals. Still later Japanese historical and heroic saga figures, Japanese writers, Koreans, Dutchmen, devils, and daily occupations and diversions of the Japanese people, masks, birds and reptiles.

The Japanese artist reproduces the most insignificant objects of every day life. One Netsuke may represent the smallest insect, another a complicated event of the heroic saga of the Shintoist and Buddhist mythology. Like a carefree happy child he tries his skill, his patience, his fancy, and his humor upon almost everything. It is most interesting to compare what the Netsuke artist produces and what he eliminates, what he often and what he seldom takes for subjects. Six of the seven gods of fortune are treated with a humor, with a lack of respect which is astonishing, but a Netsuke that represents the transformation of God to man, the Buddha Amitabha is yet to be seen. On the other hand, the merciful goddess of love, Kwannon, is occasionally produced. The artist likewise avoids bringing into existence the ruling powers, the Shogun and the mystical Mikado, for whom he apparently has a very marked respect. The figures of Geisha, or of the demi-mondaines, who completely ruled the color wood carving, are seldom seen. The pillow, rice pounder, rope, basket (Plate V, 3) and other household articles are represented, but Brockhous has never seen the religious symbols standing on the altar of the shintoist divine service; nor the holy glass, the emblem of the Shinto God Amaterasu, nor the sacred Gohei, strips of paper, upon which the divinity descends. On the other hand, one often finds the Chinese holy crystal ball which is one of the three symbols of the imperial power in Shintoism. In the Behrens collection is a Christ-like Netsuke, a Crucifixion of Christ, a copy of the figurative or plastic representation introduced by the Hollanders. Hart possessed a Netsuke of Ten-ko representing the portrait of George III in an oval medallion, carved from an English coin. Reproductions of reptiles and flying animals such as frogs, toads, owls, sea-gulls, wasps, octopus, crabs, turtles, rats, monkeys (Plate XII) and many others, are always to be found. From the animals living in Japan, the following are apparently missing: the mole, the bear, the otter, the seal, the walrus, the beautifully colored jelly-fish, the star-fish, the sea-urchin, and

the proverbial crossbill. Roosters (Plates IV, 4;
IX, 2), quails, and snakes are reproduced often, but
the duck, salamander and the much beloved night-
ingale are seldom seen. The cicada, the grass-
hopper, the glow-worm, the silk-worm or its
cocoon, and the beautiful butterfly are reproduced.
Is this at all connected with the mythological, religious meaning of animals or with their scarcity?
Of the animals of which the Bodhisatva regen-
erated, there are used: the snake, elephant (Plate
III, 3), lion (Plate III, 1), antelope, hare, horse
(Plate IV, 5), steer (Plate IV, 3), monkey, boar,
dog (Plate IV, 2), jackal (wolf), rat, tree-frog,
rooster, parrot, quail, goose, drake and the mythical griffin. These buddhist animals are seldom
seen: the lizard, peacock, partridge, pigeon (Plate
XIII, 4), woodpecker, hawk or crow.

The representatives of the Chinese animal circle
have all been reproduced as well as those of the
day and the night: the mouse, ox, tiger, hare (or
rabbit), dragon, snake, horse, goat (or ram),
monkey, cock, dog and boar. Among these there
are animals such as the tiger, the elephant, the lion
and the goat, which the Japanese had not seen and
which remained long unknown to them, so that the

reproduction of these animals has always been considered as from Chinese models. The mythological creatures on the other hand, like the dragon, the half frog, half turtle, "the noblest animal form: a hart body, dragon head and lion mane, the symbol of extreme goodness," have been taken from India through China and Korea.

It is very characteristic of carvers in general to give preference in the reproduction of an object to its humorous and even satirical side whenever possible.

In order to be able to judge which objects within his field of vision the Japanese carver preferred to select for his work and which he eliminated it is necessary to be better acquainted with the whole history, saga, and mythology of Japan than we have been heretofore.

When we study the development of Netsuke carving a little more closely, we find at first that the big gap which exists between the productions of the so-called high-art and art handicraft, as it is known in Europe, has not existed in Japan. Both are according to their nature, decorative, or ornamental, the difference between them being more quantitative than qualitative. As in Europe, the representatives of high art in Japan look down upon the Netsuke carver, the "artisan," due to a prejudice which in Japan is even less justifiable than in Europe, for the true artist and the gifted artisan are twin brothers, one of whom, from the height of his god-favored art world and exquisite taste cannot look down contemptuously upon the other as a "working slave" with "coarse" senses.

Japan does not know that terrible expression "art handicraft," which to Europeans means so much, nor does it know the meaning of it as we do.   For with us, according to a clever expression of Professor Brinckmann, the expression "art-handicraft" means "the production of unnecessary ornaments," whereas in Japan it designates the "artistic reproduction of useful and indispensable articles."   While on the one hand it has a deeper meaning in Japan, on the other hand its use directs towards development and upbuilding. This fact should not be left out of the question in judging the Japanese "art craft."   If a Japanese Mark Twain were writing on "art handicraft," he would not find himself burdened with miles and miles of pictures, but instead he would have reason to complain of the fact that it is impossible to find even the simplest object without being stirred by its beauty and artistic form.

In Europe, since the middle ages, painting and sculpture, in an endeavor to make reproductions as close to nature as possible, have far outstripped "handicraft" but the reverse is true in Japan and in entire Eastern Asia. There the "handicraft" and the ability to imitate nature very closely is already highly developed, while painting is still in its first swaddling clothes. The latter remains behind in many respects, or at least its development is onesided, while plastic art and handicraft follow their natural course in their own fashion. In painting the most idealistic style, in plastic above all things the attempt to truly reproduce nature; on the one hand absence of sky and line perspective, the lack of light and deep shadows; on the other hand, fullest understanding and observation, complete control of everything pertaining to drawing; on the one hand pure decorative surface work without substantial qualities, on the other hand the most complete execution and closest observation of anatomy and structure except in the form of human beings and sucking animals. That this is not a mere accident need not be pointed out in view of the comprehensive nature of Japanese creations. We have very good proofs of the premeditation shown in the artistic productions of those personages who at the same time were painters, sculptor and Netsuke carvers. The most prominent names are those of men who were known as painters and at the same time as Netsuke artists, as for instance; the painter and sculptor Nono-guchi Ryu-ho and a Sumarai O-gawa Ritsu-o; further the painters of the Kano school and holders of the famous Hogan and Hokkyo titles: O-ga ta, Ko-rin, Yoshi-mura, Shu-zan, Shu-getsu and others.

Even though up to the present day, the human body has received very conventional treatment in all the Japanese schools of painting, keeping more or less at a distance from nature with the intention of indicating only that which is supposed to represent fantasy and to give free play to it, as in the life-size wooden temple guards (Ni-o) in the Kofukuji temple of Nara, the Japanese statues no more represent the exact likeness of a certain individual, or a portrait in the modern sense of the word, than do the old Egyptian masterpieces. A

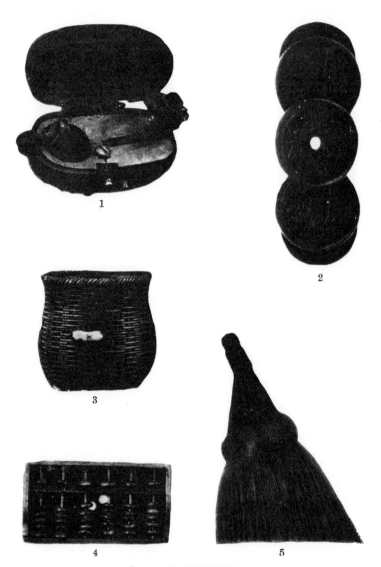

PLATE V—UTENSILS

1. Flint and Steel, (iron). 2. Coins, (wood). 3. Basket, (bone).
4. Abacus, (ivory). 5. Broom, (wood).

smaller plastic art, namely the Netsuke carving,
which is executed by another class of artists, shows
a most perfect comprehension of nature. An
anatomical lecture could be given over an ivory
Netsuke six cm. in height, which represents a skele-
ton of Asahi Gyoku-zan. Characteristic movements of human figures (Plate II, 2, 5), like those
of a dancing person, a blind man, a hero, a god, a
speaking likeness of the face-expression of a come-
dian's mask are reproduced in Japanese art as
they are in no art of any other country. Monkeys,
dogs, birds and frogs can be found nowhere in the
world equal to those of the Netsukes in so far as
delicacy and striking resemblance to nature are
concerned.

On the other hand there are a great many Netsukes that show no signs of a careful observation
of nature. Gods and heroes, animals and plants
(Plate XIV, 1), are made with more archaic
roughness, and apparently undeveloped technique
so that the original model is hardly recognizable.
Closer observation of these reproductions not only
shows defective skill but also an attempt at copying
old Chinese as well as Indian models, and furthermore, that this certain conventional style is only

applied to those objects suited for the religious
ceremonies of Indian or Chinese Buddhism,
Taoism or Confucianism. For instance, the
crane is always made in conventional style,
the heron always in his natural form. Also
the goat is produced in a conventional manner
as this animal had long been known to the
Chinese artists who carved and painted, before
it was introduced into Japan a relatively short
time ago. Almost everything that has any
connection with mythology, religion, saga, has
its symbol in Chinese art—sun and moon, man
and horse, and tiger, tree, rocks and waves have an
unchangeable type which the artist follows without thinking of making an imitation of nature.
This use of conventional types is not the work of a
people living in a state of nature who retain the
stable, ordinary, current forms of nature in their
works, but an intentional reproduction of the unusual, the special and the individual which,
through centuries and centuries of repetition has
acquired a certain sacredness. This is shown in
the selection of certain animals and certain
postures like a steer lying down (Plate IV, 3), a
lion sitting or lying with head lifted, (Plate III,

1), a tiger crouching with his head turned backwards.

Reproductions from the domain of the old Japanese religion, Shintoism, are not made in this conventional style, nor are those intended for world use and yet, persons, animals and plants are conventionally reproduced when they represent illustrations of old Chinese or Japanese fables.

We can hardly determine the great beauty of the colors of painted Netsukes by means of analogy, because the wooden Netsukes of olden times, which were painted, today show only the traces of some of the most lasting colors. There is no reason whatever why we should not be willing to admit that the Netsukes formerly showed the same beautiful, harmonious colors, unsurpassed to this day, as the beautiful woodcarvings of a Harunobu or Utamoro of the same period. In order to be influenced by the colors alone, without being enchanted by the beauty of form, it is sufficient to put one of those colored woodcarvings on its head, and you will then enjoy such a harmony of color as has never been known elsewhere in the history of art. We may conclude that the more delicate colors and tones of Netsukes shipped to

Europe have worn away through use, and there are probably some very valuable pieces in the hands of Japanese that show colors comparable to those obtained by wood-printing.

The Japanese are not satisfied with exhibiting a statue, an Okimono, or a Netsuke on the side that shows when the object stands upright; they take especial care to make the side, which is to show as decorative and beautiful as possible without failing to take the greatest pains with the work on the reverse and under sides of the object.   They finish every side so completely and perfectly that no-where can traces of work be discovered.   In European art, all the work is spent on the front side of the object; the reverse side must be contented with the poorest and most imperfect execution.   It may be that the Japanese does not always execute the reverse and under sides with the same care as the show side, but he certainly never neglects them (Plates V, 3; XIII, 3; XIV, 6).

The necessity of representing the beauty of proportion is always either consciously or unconsciously before the eyes of the Japanese.   This of course tends to give his plastic works much more charm.   One thing that cannot be found in Japanese art which often appears in modern western art, is an out-stretched arm. This is just as ugly as the broad basis of a figure with a narrow top, or the polygonal empty spaces between the limbs of certain figures.

The mistake of our artists in attiring modern people in antique clothing, could not possibly be made by the Japanese. Neither would it occur to him—in spite of the Indo-Chinese representations —to attempt to characterize in an allegoric figure, a person for whom he has any liking, merely by giving him all sorts of attributes. In European art a nude man provided with a wheel can represent "industry," the "workman," the "railroad guard," or a "man-at-arms." The characteristic facial expression for which our art is so much praised is in reality completely lacking when compared to the Asiatic plastic art. To the European a nude female figure,—unless the label or catalogue of the "International Art Exhibition" states the contrary, represents a "Venus." When provided with an anchor it represents "navigation" or "hope"; and with an apple in the hand "Eve." A more or less naked man with an apple in his hand is a "Paris."

In Japan the symbol is in the figure itself, and a jovial figure of a man with naked stomach becomes a god of fortune or the children's friend Hotei, the chubby-cheeked stupidly smiling face of a maiden, is an Uzume (Plate VI, 6), or the man with a high forehead personifies the god of fortune Fukurokuju (Plate X, 2; XIII, 4). The Japanese came very near acquiring also the intricate characterizations of later Buddhism, because the simple Buddha figure was introduced into Japan to represent Buddhism one thousand years after its originator, Gautama!

The following remain symbolic for Japanese art as well as for Indian art; the vadjra, the wheel, the priest's sprinkling brush, the dish for receiving the blood of the victim, etc. and Japanese art also adopted the "disciples of the lord," the rakan, the Indian attributes (sprinkling brush, book, slingshot) and the symbolic postures (hands folded—meditation, uplifted right—science, etc.) and the enlarged ear-lap of the Buddhist saints and the Deva. It is possible that the leaf-apron, the curling or long straight hair and the round wide-open eyes of the white race could not be adopted as attributes. But in that case they belong to the heterogeneous classes. The leaf-apron is not only worn by the Sennin but also by the taoistic spirits and the barbarians, as for instance the Tartarians. The Hollanders (Plate IX, 2; XVI, 1), as well as the Indian and mythological long-armed and long-legged (Plate XVIII, 4; X, 4), Ashinaga and Tenaga have curly hair. Long straight hair designates all kinds of supernatural beings. The fish-tail mermaid, the dwarf and the mad spirit, have round eyes, which perhaps points to Arjan or Malayan, and possibly to Central-Chinese origin.

In the handling of detail the art of the Japanese Netsuke stands way above the achievements of all other people. We also have had periods in which detail attained its full artistic value; we may say that the greatest painters, not only have not condemned the reproduction of minute details, but have sought for absolute perfection in detail in contrast to the other artists of their epoch, who were also inferior to them in many other ways. Most of the painters and great sculptors from the Renaissance on, handle details superficially although examples of the contrary can be found as well in the Renaissance as among the Greeks. What infinite charm is attached to the small Japanese carvings which, although meant to be effective from a distance, become doubly attractive when looked at closely. The deepening of the draperies, the pattern of the clothing, the texture of the soft animal hair, and the force in the facial expression which increases tremendously under the magnifying glass, strengthen the characteristics at close observation without spoiling in any way the effect from a distance. The Japanese, like the Greek masters of naturalistic genre, are aware of the fact that detail is highly necessary to attain the ideal.

The ideal of the Japanese nobles and warriors was disdain for sensual pleasure and increasing willingness for a fearless death; the ideal of the other classes, however, is joy of living, harmless pleasure, happiness on earth and in heaven.

Just as the frequent earthquakes of Japan have determined its architectural development and art, and also possibly the use of the tough wood and the low building, so in its turn has this low style of architecture given its painting, its plastic art— with very few exceptions—and its handicraft, a miniature character.

The Chinese have always been the connecting

link between Japan and the rest of the civilized world. In the 1st and 2nd centuries A. D., they learned to know the Buddhist and Religious art productions in Gandhara, closely beheld the Greco-Buddhist type, and introduced it into Korea during the 5th century and into Japan during the 7th century.

In fact, Japanese sculpture springs from a warm love for Nature. One mark of distinction is that the Japanese sculptor, wherever he has his free choice, prefers the reproduction of motion to that of rest. No other people in the world have shown such keen desire for reproducing dramatic movement as the Japanese. That Japanese art thereby enters into competition with the creators of the Laokoon group, is not surprising. "Motion, we fear, could prejudice the truth, and we therefore mistrust it as we do something dangerous, something destructive. Motion is to be found everywhere in Japanese art, in architecture, sculpture, drawing. The artist resists rest, equilibrium, even lines, absolute order. But he is such a thorough observer, that he can analyze a motion and grasp phases of it which to us are wholly unknown. His object is not, like ours, to represent happiness, love, pain, belief; his element is fighting, excitement, comedy, tragedy," (Ary Renan). The plastic masterpieces intended for divine service, which from olden times down to this day have represented personifications of peace and harmony, are not to be overlooked in this connection. The self-less rest of a Buddha has never been so perfectly characterized in figure and countenance by any other Asiatic people—with the exception of the Chinese—as by the Japanese! Little or nothing is known in Europe about real Chinese art. One thing is certain, however, that all great Japanese painters and sculptors of religious subjects have received their inspiration from the old Chinese masterpieces of art in Nara and Horiuchi.

It must be mentioned however that the high-born Japanese of our day looks at the "art of the people" to which the Netsukes belong, from over his shoulder, or at least has heretofore done so. In his eyes art is only art when it inclines towards the strongly defined Chinese and Korean models.

The Netsuke artist chooses the object which he wishes to make a reproduction of; a moment of occurrence which is eminently characteristic, a

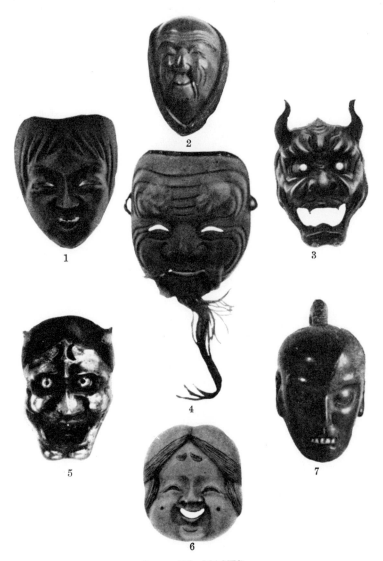

PLATE VI—MASKS

1. No Mask, (wood).   2. Man's Face, (nut).   3. No Mask, (wood).
4. No Mask, (lacquered wood).   5. Mask, (metal).   6. No
Mask, (ivory).   7. Death's Head, (lacquered wood).

pose which must be interpreted as the most pro-
lific imaginable.

Another peculiarity of the Japanese artist may
be mentioned here. Take a Netsuke representing
a chestnut, for instance, upon which a little monkey
is seated looking for a movable and partly visible
worm which is hiding inside the chestnut. Both
the worm and the chestnut are of natural size
whereas the monkey is made smaller than the chestnut, even though the latter is in reality thirty
times as large (Plate II, 1). Then there is the
Netsuke representing a man lying on his back at-
tempting to hold with his arms, chin and legs a
slippery eel which is twice as long as the man himself, and if alive, would be about nine feet long!
The enlarging of the chestnut, the worm and the
eel has been done purposely. In the first case this
was done to symbolize the gigantic amazement of
the monkey over that mysterious something which
is hidden inside the chestnut; in the other case to
represent the tremendous amount of labor the
hungry fisherman is undergoing in order to catch
the slippery eel.

An artist often selects an object that has been
selected a thousand times before, or is within his

circle of vision that fills the available space, or which can be most characteristically executed in the material to be used. But the execution is always new. The artist returns to nature and discovers on a knotty excrescence which he wants to use, points of contact between his conception and the material on hand. He labors with incredible patience to correlate his material and his idea, using all the materials which are at his disposal; gold, silver, lead, lacquer, steel, iron and mother of pearl, to create leaves and stems, or water or birds, clouds or moonlight, sunshine or shadows, little men or women.

According to the object's requirements he carves, now superficially, now deeply, at one time suggestively, at another in detail, conventionally or naturally. He works fast or slowly, polishes, paints, paints again and polishes again, puts the Netsuke in water or acid for days or months until it is ready, absolutely ready, not too little or not too much of anything, because, according to his own conception, "perfect execution" alone means art!

The classic Japanese creations have the advantage over Western art productions in that the fight for "the right to live" which existed in the West, as well as the fight for the "right to enjoy" and the consequence, "the fight of competition," was not known to the Japanese. The Japanese artist works freely and only for himself, without giving any thought whatever to "cost of production" "publication price" and the "work time" required for the execution.

"I could probably create just as artistic a thing as a little Japanese art object" said an intelligent European architect to John LaFarge, "but where would I find the time? Even more than that, where find the time to do the necessary study and exercises required for this work? All I can do is to project a plan, have it executed, and close my eyes over the result! I should only be mildly criticized because I have not accomplished more than my duty. But doing more than one's duty is the real beginning of art, and therefore every little Japanese art production is a greater work of art than a modern cathedral." This judgment of the architect although exaggerated, is based upon the right idea. Because the measure which we are in the habit of using to judge art and artistic skill, is a false one. In order to prove that a work of art is complete, we must first learn to understand, that "rules of harmony" exist for our eyes as well as for our ears. Should these laws some day be thoroughly mastered for art as they are for music, then and only then shall we have found the way which will enable us to determine and classify the real artists of all times, and decide their rank, always in accordance with the degree of our instinctive following of these rules of artistic harmony. Then will the Japanese Netsuke carver be given the place to which he is entitled by right.

CHAPTER IV

NETSUKE COLLECTIONS

THE fast growing wish of the Netsuke collector
to know the history of the objects of his devotion,
the conditions under which they originated, the
ideas they embody, and the life of the artist who
created them, in our case, cannot be given complete
satisfaction.

There is very little German literature on Japanese art available, and none at all on Netsukes in
particular. In the Western literature little can
be found on the Japanese artists and the history of
their life. Even the Japanese literature on Netsukes is very scanty. This is partly because the
Japanese considered the artist an impersonal
being, who only lived within his work, partly because the Japanese heretofore have had very little
historical interest, and partly, because the Netsuke
carver belongs to a class of artists and craftsmen
for whom the contemporary writer had no interest.

There are comparatively few collections which

were made by intelligent people soon after the Japanese art objects became known.

It is to be hoped that more and more collections will be formed to guard against the threatened disappearance of these most important examples of artistic and ethnographic carvings. Not many of us can collect paintings by Raphael, but we can afford to buy small carvings which no land has created more perfectly than Japan. In almost every large city there are importers or dealers in Japanese wares, or curiosity and antique shops, in which Netsukes can occasionally be found.

The prices which have been and are being paid for Netsukes have fluctuated tremendously. Many pieces show by their inscription that they were carved for an aristocratic wearer. Such patrons gave the famous carver a home and provided for his necessities as long as the work on a beautiful piece lasted. In many cases, this covered a period of months and even years. We know it to be a fact that some artists have been supported throughout their entire life. When Japan opened its gates to European trade in 1868, European clothes were imported, the Netsukes became superfluous and great numbers of the most valuable

pieces were sold in large quantities at most ridicul-
ous prices.

Among the European collections are many examples of bad modern work. The beginner, however, will be glad if he is able to secure so-called
"bad modern works," as he can in this way develop
his taste and eye, and gradually replace the originally acquired pieces by good ones. But the
really poorly executed Netsukes are recognized
even by the novice. Occasionally Netsukes are
offered for sale at a low price by dealers who, on
account of the small circle of buyers base the sell-
ing price on the purchase price which they acci-
dentally paid for the object and not on its intrinsic
value. A beautiful collection can still be obtained
without too much cost, by buying at occasional
public auctions from collections.

The collecting of Netsukes is not rapid; it requires patience, time, and study. The market is
overrun with rubbish, which one is obliged to ex-
amine very carefully, in order to find perhaps one
piece which will compensate him for the trouble.
But it sometimes happens that a Netsuke is found
which is signed with an unknown name, and which
would be worth being worn by the Mikado himself.

This is the compensation that is constantly beckoning to the patient colletcor and stirring his enthusiasm.

The first Netsukes came to Europe long before the time of the opening of the Japanese ports to Americans, and before the opening of the country in 1868, through Portuguese and Dutch merchants, who purchased a certain kind of Japanese lacquer work which met with the liking of Marie Antoinette and a few connoisseurs about 1780.

As far as the arrangement of Netsuke collections is concerned, it is advisable to keep them from being exposed to dust by putting them into glass cases with glass edges. Dust fills up the holes, makes the raised work coarse, kills the gloss and takes away from the carvings a great deal of their charm. When Netsukes are placed together with curios, trinkets and other objects on the mantel pieces, there is danger of their being broken by careless domestics, swept away, or even carried to an unknown destination in the folds of a woman's dress upon the occasion of a friendly visit. One of my Netsukes one evening made such a trip unbeknown to the lady who carried it through streets

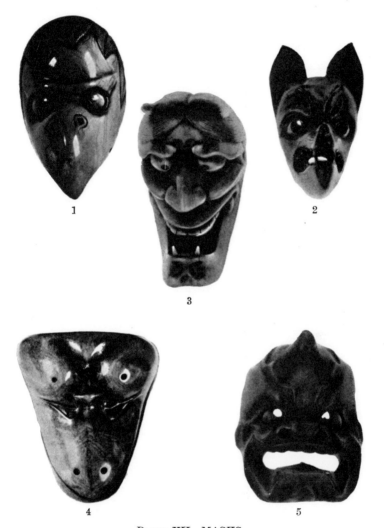

1   2

3

4   5

PLATE VII—MASKS

1. Bird's Head, (ivory). 2. No Mask, (lacquered wood). 3. No Mask,
(wood). 4. Woman's Head, (ivory). 5. No Mask, (wood).

and streets until she finally discovered it and returned it to me. The glass show cases in the museums do not seem to me to be very practical, because they are too deep; they should not be deeper than about ten cm. A case of that size will easily hold two rows of Netsukes. A mirror or green plush should be placed in the back of the cabinet.

As a matter of fact we would do much better not to expose them at all, but follow the example of the Japanese who put them under lock and key like all other art treasures, and only bring them out occassionally. But then we must have friends who share our interest. The Japanese arrange meetings in order to devote, in a most ceremonial manner, a few hours to art and to enjoy together and discuss a poem, a sword blade, or a Netsuke. "Shared pleasure is double pleasure." Where this is not possible, we can at least awaken a superficial interest and keep for ourselves the real pleasure we derive from an hour spent in looking at a few pieces, and thus developing our mind and soul.

A Netsuke collection can be arranged in many different ways. The arrangement, according to art periods can only be accomplished by those whose collection is composed of at least several hundred pieces.　If there were in existence an art history, giving the requisite definite periods, schools and their characteristics, and above all a history of the artists who worked during these respective periods, such a scheme could easily be carried out. We could then separate the carvers of ivory from the wood carvers and others who worked with various materials, provided the same artist had not often worked with many different materials.　But no such close connection existed between certain carvings of various materials, as exists between certain Netsukes made of the same material.

There is very little occasion for classification according to motives.　Many artists have restricted themselves to a limited field.　Through comparison with the production of a similar motive by another artist, we can judge to what extent the carver has attained perfection in representing nature and character and to what degree he has mastered the technique.　Perfection in artistic conception, as well as the progress of an artist's

artistic individuality compared to that of his predecessors and competitors, can be determined only
by comparison between work based on the same
motives.

It is a mistake to admire, enjoy and appraise art,
works of art and artists when removed from their
environment. We can understand and prize them
much better when we know their connections with
their home, climate and race, with mythological
and religious aspects and historical traditions,
with the artistic and professional, aesthetic and
technical knowledge and ability of their time.

A great deal may be learned by those who are interested in these peculiar carvings from the de-
scriptions of Netsukes of which there is not a single
one that is made without some allusion to Japanese
life. It will give them an understanding of this
branch of art and help them to develop it further.
In these modern times in which art prefers to take
as a subject the sad side of human life and even
goes so far as to represent things of a pathological
nature, the connoisseur of this Japanese minor art
will all the more enjoy it when he begins to understand and appreciate that which permeates this

art, namely: absolute contentment with one's self and the beautiful world, the greatest peace of mind and ingenuous and often humorous conception of even the most serious things that exist in heaven and on earth.

CHAPTER V

In pre-historic times, prior to 660 B. C., when the first emperor Jimmu Tenno is supposed to have reigned, Asiatic art was introduced into Japan from Korea. From 33 B. C. regular relations began between these two states, and during the first year before Christ was born, a decree was given out which was of great importance to the plastic art, namely that in place of the sacrifice of human beings which had been the custom established and carried out by the deceased emperor, in future only clay figures would be offered. As the Shintoist religion had no representation of gods, sculpture had been confined to the ornamentation of weapons. After the introduction of the Buddhist religion, 552 A. D., the beautiful old wooden statues came into existence in Nara on or about 600 A. D. In 749 the colossal statue of the Buddha was cast in Nara. In 794 the imperial residence was transferred to Kyoto, the palaces were decorated, and the dance and mask fashion adopted for the palaces as well as for Buddhistic ceremonies. This marks the beginning of the art of mask carving.

As early as the 10th century men of high rank busied themselves with sculpture. Two of these men created a lasting reputation for themselves. They became the originators of a family of carvers that remained famous throughout the course of many generations. They were Ko-sho and his son Jo-cho. They were descendants of emperor Koko (885 A. D.). It appears that the first prosperous period of mask carving was from the 10th-15th century. Under the Ashikaga Shoguns (1338-1573) religious carving declined.

In the year 1586 we know that Taiko Hideyoshi sent an expedition to Korea which returned to Japan with many new clever and artistic suggestions, Chinese models and even artists, which laid the ground-work for another period of prosperity in Japanese art. But it would be wrong to suppose that these artistic suggestions and models were slavishly imitated. Even though there are still a great many archaic forms to be found, the productions of Japanese sculpture are executed with a gracefulness and delicacy hitherto unknown to the Chinese world. It is certain that Japanese art handicraft received other suggestions from the south and the east, from the Malayan and Polynesian world. Like its earliest mythology, many emblems and ornaments bear signs of close relationship with the traditions and artistic peculiarities of those southern and eastern people.

Among those art objects which Japan exclusively has created and developed, the Netsukes are the most important. While until the end of the 16th century they appear to have been made, along with other things, by mask and statue carvers, they constitute from that time on a special branch of art, independent of all other arts, as do also the older Ojimes.

Brockhous does not share the opinion of Huish that the Netsukes are of Chinese origin, because in olden times they represented Chinese Saga figures, clad in Chinese clothes, and also because he came across one of these objects that was made of nephrite. On the contrary, the characteristics of a Netsuke are distinctly Japanese and surprisingly original, and they overflow with the gracefulness that only Japan can produce. However, it can not be denied that since about 1700 there have been

Netsukes that give one the impression of having been of Chinese origin. There are many Chinese carvings made of ivory and nephrite which, by adding apertures, are converted into Netsukes and worn as such. In Soken Kisho mention is made of the fact that an art similar to that of Netsuke carving is called To-bori. But this means only that the Netsukes in their perception and form were Chinese and that above all they represented the earlier Buddhistic objects in Indo-Chinese forms: elephants, tigers, lions, fabulous fantastic animals, dragons, sennins, etc. and also, peculiarly enough, the nude human female figure, of which the reproduction in Japan is indecent.

The Netsukes are an invention of the Japanese and their production is limited to Japan. Neither the East-Asiatic people, like the Manchurians, the Chinese and Koreans, nor the neighboring Asians of Annam, Tongking, Burmah, Thibet, nor the Malayans, Micronesians and Polynesians have any objects akin to Netsukes, although they too fasten certain objects to their girdle. Only one other country in the world supposedly uses similar girdle buttons, and that is Hungary! The Hungarian farmer who still wears the national costume attaches his pipe and tobacco pouch on his girdle by means of a steel Netsuke. If it is true that the Hungarians are related to the Japanese from a linguistic point of view, could it not be possible then that there has existed, from primeval times, an unknown relationship between the Japanese and Hungarian Netsukes?

The question when Netsukes were invented is a hard one to answer. It is certain however that they were not in existence in the 10th century up to the time which is represented by the famous imperial collection in the treasure palace of Nara. It may be that they date from the time of the introduction of the girdle. If through investigations it can be ascertained when the change in the Japanese wearing apparel took place and at what time the girdle became fashionable for men as well as for women, it is possible that in this way we may discover when the people began to carry useful articles on the obi and at the same time something about the invention of Netsukes. It is said that the Kojiki, which is the "Pentateuch" of the Japanese, mentions in one of its parts that the wearing of the girdle followed the publication of this book, on or about 712 A. D.

The first Netsukes probably were made out of a queerly shaped piece of root, which on account of its peculiarity attracted the finder, who gave the object the name which it retained later. Also small dried bottle gourds partly lacquered, animal teeth and the like are supposed to have been put to this use ever since the early ages.

It is said that the button was first made hollow on one side for the purpose of using it as an extended holder for smouldering ashes which are carried outside the house for lighting pipes etc. Netsukes, however, existed before the cultivation of tobacco began in 1605. Furthermore, among old wooden Netsukes, Brockhous has never found one that has shown any traces of burns such as we find in the bowl of our briar pipes. But there is a special shell-shaped kind of Netsuke, which is used to contain the smouldering tobacco ashes (Plate I, 1). Poor men are said to still use them. They were called Suigaraake, which means "Tobacco ashes" (suigara) "a thing used for emptying" (ake) or Hihataki which means "Fire" (hi) "extinguisher" (hataki). These articles were made of copper, silver, cloisonne and eventually of wood and ivory.

Most likely the Manjus (Plate I, 1, 2, 3), the smooth, flat, round buttons measuring from two and one-half to seven and one-half cm. in diameter and one cm. thick made of wood, and decorated like a Netsuke preceded the figure Netsuke. These are most artistically made and in the selection of the material, work, color, and form suit the character and the profession of the wearer and also match the decorated articles for which they were intended. According to Brinkley the Netsuke is only a further development of the Ojime, which originally was used to attach the Sagemono to the girdle. This theory that the figure Netsuke followed the Manju which was in turn preceded by the Ojime has much to commend it.

The artistic preparation began in the 15th century under the luxurious and elegant Shogun Yoshimasa. As early as the 8th and 10th century some names of mask carvers were mentioned and it is not at all impossible that these artists had made carved masks of small dimensions, like the Netsuke masks (Plate VI.). At the end of the 15th century, about the time of Ashikaga Shogun Yoshimasa (1436-90), the Netsuke was supposed to be used as a button to hold in the girdle small

bags for flint and steel, writing material, small
bags, and the usual inro. At a later date, after
the introduction of tobacco, the Netsukes were only
used to attach the leather tobacco pouch, the leather
pipe case and the Sagemono. Since the beginning
of the 17th century, Netsukes were mostly used by
merchants and workmen, to attach their smoking
utensils. Every Japanese smoked, but not every
Japanese felt the necessity of carrying writing
articles, seals or medicine boxes. Surprisingly
enough, in Europe the Netsukes are only used in
connection with the latter. The tobacco articles,
which are only worn on the girdle by men, are
usually attached on the left side of the body and
the Inro on the right side. The last named object, judging from its name (in-seal, stamp, ro-
small basket) originally must have been a container for a seal, a key and also money. The custom of stamping a signature on a document, in
order to assure its genuineness began during the
first years of the 17th century. Later on it became a requisite for the validity of all contracts,
and from the beginning of the Tokugawa period
(1603) all legal papers had to be sealed by the head
of the family whether they concerned him or any

other member of his household. Ever since that time the seal and pad have belonged to a class of ever ready articles used by every merchant, doctor, employee, etc. In the Kei-cho period (1596-1611) the same quadratic round or oblong form was adopted for medicine boxes as for stamp boxes; they were executed in lacquered wood, and given the name of Inro, which has since been used exclusively to designate medicine boxes. From the beginning of the Tokugawa period, medicine boxes were worn generally by the Samurai, mostly on the Manju. This fashion was naturally adopted later by the other classes. In the beginning of the 18th century the Inros were being worn less and less, most people used them only as ornaments on ceremonial occasions. This was very fortunate for the collector, as otherwise the beautiful lacquer which they still retain would have been worn off.

"Southern Barbarians," such as the Portuguese, brought the plant, which they called tobacco, into Japan about 1570, and the name was preserved there after the cultivation of this product had begun in 1605. Men and women soon were so won over to this delightful means of enjoyment that the Shogun Iyeyasu in 1612 was obliged to completely prohibit smoking as well as further development of the cultivation of tobacco! But this drastic measure could not be maintained for long. Even at the present day there is not a single people that practises smoking so generally as the Japanese. Nevertheless they are not such "steady smokers" as we Europeans are. Their little pipe which is half the size of a small thimble only allows a very few but joyful draughts from a sort of blond thread-fine tobacco. The smoke is "inhaled" very slowly and blown out through the nose. On the occasion of visits as well as during shopping, the tobacco box and tea are presented. On the other hand the introduction of fire arms in 1542 or 1544, which brought about a greater change in all feudal relations than the cultivation of tobacco, has not produced any similar art.

Women carried their tobacco articles in the girdle folds, but hung their silver miniature medicine box only on their girdle and attached it with a Netsuke.

The oldest Netsukes still in existence date from the end of the 16th century. But Huish frankly states that he has not succeeded in finding any one who had seen them. Most of the Netsukes that

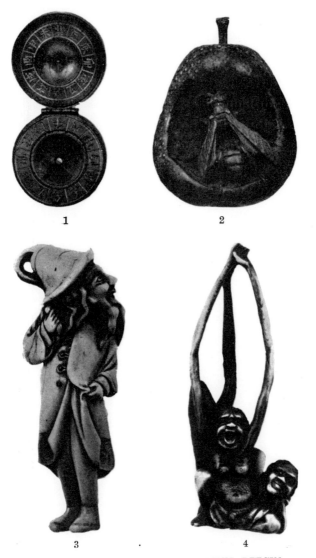

PLATE VIII—COMPASS AND OTHER PIECES

1. Sun Dial and Compass, (metal). 2. Pear and Wasp, (wood) 3
Dutchman, (wood). 4. Long-armed man, (ivory).

are still on hand were produced from the 17th
to the 19th century.

It is impossible to predict what effect Western
art will have upon the development which took
place in the Meiji period. It is not at all improb-
able however that the incomparable universal artistic gift of the Japanese people will produce
geniuses who will surpass the accomplishments in
art of the rest of the world, just as the ingenious
masters of the Greeks and of the Renaissance
period sprang from an art gifted people who surpassed in their work everything that had been produced up to their time.

As far as we can ascertain, the political and
social developments of the Tokugawa-Shoguns and
the demand for luxury by their successors, beginning with Iyemitsu in 1623, are the causes of the
great perfection shown in the many art creations
in which the Japanese have surpassed the rest of
the world. Their victorious course began at the
end of the 17th century, with the Genroku period;
painting, carving in wood, ivory and bamboo, wood
printing, potter ware, lacquer ware and articles
inlaid with gold, silver and mother of pearl, metal
works, cloisonne, alloys of a special kind, swords

and sword ornaments, silk weaving and silk dye-
ing, paper manufacture, etc.

Political and psychological motives moved the
Shogun of the Tokugawa Dynasty, namely its first
members, to favor art. Iyeyasu, the first Tokugawa, had definitely brought to an end the five
hundred year war; but the wild, daring, war-like
spirit remained within many who had spent their
entire life preparing for war and fighting. It was
therefore necessary to create some sort of diversion,
and Iyeyasu who was one of the most thorough
students of human nature, suggested the development of art for the preservation of peace. However, he made certain rules which maintained the
desire for war-like glory and ability, so that Japan,
after two hundred and fifty years of absolute
peace, still retained its reputation as a thoroughly
war-like nation. And during all that time every
branch of art and literature flourished. This is
the accomplishment of a single man whose like no
other country has ever produced. The most beautiful things that Japan ever created and that show
the most complete development of nature and art,
are the temples in Nikko, which have been conse-
crated to the memory of this man.

About the civil relations of all these artists and handicraft workers, the architects of that period as well as of the present day, we know very little. Doubless, in later times, many of them were merchants, whose business was handed down from father to son.

In earlier times, the artists had never been merchants or workmen by profession, but served in a princely family, from whom they obtained a home, clothing and support for themselves and their families, also perhaps a little house of their own and a small garden; they lived without care for the future, without wants, without avarice, but only with their art and their love of nature. The complete happiness with which they devoted themselves to their art is the best proof of this.

On the other hand, most of this history is incomplete, as it gives only the names of the Netsuke masters. They belonged to a class of people who were separated from the literary world, to which belonged the painter, but not the class of wood carver-painters known in the West, like Utamaro, Toyokuni, Hokusai. Up to 1750 the artists presumably were courtiers of the Shogun, Buddhist priests or Noblemen, also men of education, breed-

ing and position. With Matahei, the originator
of the Ukiyoye, a new element is brought into the
art, namely the civil artist and art craftsman, who
work for fame as well as for money.

Whether some Netsuke carvers had founded a
guild or a corporation of which they were members, is not known. We know that there were some
whose only profession was Netsuke carving, but
that the greatest part of the carvers exercised their
art only occasionally and in a dilettante fashion.

That it was the carvers of the Buddhist cult
objects mentioned heretofore who were the first
ones to decorate the buttons which, up to that time,
had been made without ornament, appears, according to Huish to have resulted from the fact
that most of the Netsukes represented the figures
of human beings. It is stated in Soken Kisho that
the first Netsuke carvers were wood-cutters, who
formerly made false sets of teeth from box-tree
wood. Only two tooth technicians who were also
Netsuke carvers are named: Ne-goro So-kyu and
Kame-ya Hi-go.

According to the book of Yokoi, it appears that
the Netsuke masks were made by the same famous
carvers who brought into existence the life size

theatre masks, and furthermore, that the figure
Netsukes were made by the same carvers who
manufactured wooden dolls for children.

There is perhaps also some relation between the
Netsuke carvers and the Xylographers, to whom
we owe the famous Japanese color wood printing.
The period in which they flourished, from 1700-
1840 and especially between 1765 and 1810, coincides with that of Netsukes.   Consequently it is
possible that the artist of the Ukiyoye period, con-
sidering the similarity of the material and instruments used, created both arts.   It is also possible
that as Xylographers they were known under a
different name than as Netsuke carvers.

Noblemen have also been carvers. The Japanese
nobles were only hunters and warriors; it was considered unsuitable for them to busy themselves
with commerce or agriculture.   But a nobleman,
even a prince, who laid aside his sword to pick up
paint brush or chisel, did not disgrace his title;
on the contrary, he acquired thereby a brilliant
name as an artist and lasting fame.   An artistic
masterpiece probably brought some men more
fame than the severed head of an enemy during
wartime.   Any one, who, thanks to his talent, be-

came a member of the household of a Daimyo (prince) might be knighted, and all those who carried two swords were placed on an equal basis. There are dilettantes, who on account of their great artistic ability are supposed to have been granted the title of a prince, such as Kami, or another high title like Kogen.

There are families like De-me, Kiku-gawa, O-no, Shiba-yama and others, who, from generation to generation have devoted themselves to the art of carving Netsukes, although the bearing of the same family name, which we so often find, is the result of this Japanese custom of the adoption of a suitable assistant by the master, or of the son-in-law by the head of the family. Once Brockhous came across the signature De-me Sha-chu Shige-mitsu, which means that Shige-mitsu signs as a member of the De-me "Corporation" or "Club" or "School."

Occasionally there are Netsukes which have been made by the joint efforts of two artists.

The pupil in Netsuke schools was obliged during the course of several years to exercise himself in copying models by older masters or by his own masters, making from ten to twelve copies of each object, before the master passed his judgment on them. After about ten years of hard work, from seven o'clock in the morning until ten o'clock in the evening, the pupil usually received the privilege of acquiring one sign or syllable of his master's name for the future, so that, for instance, the pupil of Masa-nobu can call himself Masa-michi. This transferring of names was celebrated by gifts offered to the master, his family, to the "oldest friends" and to the servants. Then the new master returned to his home and opened a school, where were copied objects that he used to copy himself as well as his own creations.

This perhaps explains the many copies of one subject and its innumerable minor details which have been made in the course of many centuries, although none of them were imitated in a servile way. In cases where it is impossible to ascertain whether a Netsuke comes from a master about whom it is said that he was the inventor of the object in question, they are not necessarily of inferior quality, even though they may be school productions. It is of far greater importance for the collector to know that an object is a perfect reproduction of Shu-zan than to know whether or not that particular piece has been created by that

famous carver.   A great many so called, marked
and unmarked Netsukes of Shu-zan are in circula-
tion.   Brockhous has not yet seen one that was
certainly genuine and therefore could be held up
as a proof and vindication of his world wide
reputation.   A similar case is that of the Netsukes
which are marked with the famous name Mi-wa,
found among all collections.   It is therefore highly
necessary to make up lists of those prominent
artists who at one time could only be insufficiently
identified.   The eleven most famous artists are,
according to Huish; Shu-zan, Mi-wa, I'-kuan,
Masa-nao, Tomo-tada, Tada-toshi, De-me U-man,
De-me Je-man, Min-ko, Tomo-chika, Ko-kei.   But
one glance through the list of artists names which
Brockhous has compiled shows that the name Min-
ko represents five artists, to say nothing of the fact
that nobody is in a position to prove whether the
objects mentioned in connection therewith are
carved by Min-ko or copied from Min-ko's models.

According to Professor Yokoi the most famous
of all famous carvers is O-gasa-wara I'-sai of
Wakayama (prominent from 1781-88) and the
most famous carvers are: Hina-ya Ryu-ho (1595-
1669), Izumi-ya Tomo-tada (before 1781), and

Seibe-i (before 1781) of Kyoto; Hogen Yoshi-mura Chu-zan (before 1781), Un-judo Shu-me-maru (before 1781), Hogen Hi-guchi Shu-getsu (before 1781) of Osaka; lastly Min-ko of Tsu.

We know little also of the dwelling place of the carvers. As Gonse says: "It seems that the place called Uji, situated close by the old Mikado town of Nara has from olden times possessed a monopoly of carvings. For a long time Uji remained the center of this product." Uji is situated near Kyoto, and neither Gonse nor the Soken Kisho gives artists who have lived in Uji, whereas it is known that from the year 1135 up to the present time the so-called "Nara Ningyo," small wooden statues, have been made in Nara by the Himonoshi. "In the middle of the 18th century various artists' studios came into existence in Kyoto and Yedo, which successfully brought to an end the fight with the older Nara. Ever since that time Kyoto has been the center of the Netsuke carving in ivory and wood, after it had been transferred from Tokyo" (Gonse). According to Griffis and Brinkley, the most prominent Netsuke carvers are supposed to have lived in the three capitals: Yedo, Kyoto and Osaka.

The year 1603, during which peace descended upon Japan with Tokugawa Shogun Iyeyasu after four hundred and fifty years of civil war, may be considered the birth year of national art. The first flourishing period of national art and also of the Netsuke carving developed about that time and lasted until the end of the Hoyei period (1710). A second flourishing period is the Shotoku (1711-15) to the Horeki (1751-63) period. Artistic creation in all branches reached its highest development from the Meiwa period (1764-71) to the Bunkwa (1804-17), which marks the end of the second period of Netsuke art. A third period begins with the Bunsei (1818-29) and continues to the Kayei period (1848-53).

THIRD PERIOD 1818-1853

The greatest number of Netsukes in existence were produced during this third period. Probably many carvings whose signature and form point to the 18th century, were only made in the beginning of the 19th century by famous, skillful imitators, and by pupils of earlier schools, who copied old models which were in fashion. Many collectors decidedly prefer the ivory carvings of the 19th century to those of earlier periods.

An absolute separation between the second and third period is hardly possible, but the end of the third period can be very accurately determined, as it coincides with the end of Japan's exclusion from the rest of the world, and the introduction of modern European and American so-called civilization. Although the importation of Western articles had continually increased during the course of several years prior to the landing of Commodore Perry in Gore Hama, in 1853, this incident marks the beginning of the enormous flood of good and bad articles from the industries, and workshops of the Western nations which for many years supplanted the beautiful antiques of Japan. However, it appears that during the last few years Japan has returned to the old idea of appreciating the value and the superiority of national artistic talent. The Japanese have gone back to their own art but without rejecting modern science and technique. When shorter hours of work and increased cost of labor and materials express their opinion, art always becomes more taciturn. It may be that the godly heaven of Izanagi and

Izanami has another conception and will awaken new genius to stave off the complete oblivion which is threatening this wonderful art.

Reports on carvers of this period are yet to be collected, because tradition still has the upper hand with the people. If new Japan has acquired, with the other modern improvements, the desire for studying historical development, we have reason to hope that some day we shall learn more about this interesting class of people, and this is of great importance for the preservation and propagation of artistic creation among the mass of the people.

It seems that since the middle of the 19th century the carving of Netsukes had begun to decline. Beautiful although mechanical copies of good old Netsukes are constantly being produced by the modern artist, in an attempt to fill the demands that are overrunning the market. Large decorative carvings (Okimono) are being made for the export trade. What the carving gains in size, it loses in originality and force. There are also Okimonos which could be called classic for that kind of art. It frequently happens that a decorative carving which shows at the first glance that

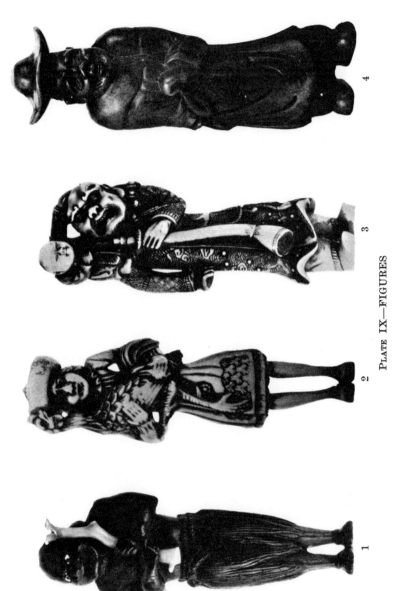

PLATE IX—FIGURES

1. Mythological figure, (wood and coral). 2. Dutchman with rooster, (ivory). 3. Man and child, (ivory). 4. Priest (wood).

it was not meant to be worn as a Netsuke, is easily converted into one by adding the two holes. I call these artificial Netsukes: Okimono-Netsukes. It cannot be denied that the modern Okimonos are exceedingly attractive artistic objects. These modern carvings in ivory and wood far outdo, as far as gracefulness and artistic perfection is concerned, all American and European articles of the kind, that are produced at the present day.

On account of the change in the style of modern Japanese society, a similar fate has befallen many of the other artistically executed articles that are of Japanese origin. Like the Netsukes, the Inros, swords, pipe cases, silk garments and satin dresses find only a very narrow market, since European attire has been adopted by the Japanese Court and the fashionable world. With them, most of the art objects of the Japanese household have disappeared in the hurricane of modernism, engulfed by the irresistible though slow oppression of style. The beautiful lacquer utensils in the capitals are replaced by modern furniture of European origin, the Makimono and Kakemono by Western chromos.

Brinkley, however, believes that there are today

dozens of artists who can make Netsukes which are not at all inferior to the products of famous masters of earlier times, if they only had sufficient encouragement and could receive a proper price. Their talent is at present directed towards Okimonos "but it is not to be supposed that they are a whit inferior to the old-time experts in conception and execution."

CHAPTER VI

WHOSOEVER derives pleasure from an attractive object of Asiatic art and is interested in knowing whether it is of Indian, Siamese, Thibetan, Chinese or Japanese origin, must not overlook the marks which are placed in such concealed spots that they appear sometimes as the decoration on a dress, an ornament on a torus, or even more casually. Western art craft productions, except Keramics, never bear the name of the artist or artisan. It may be that this is due to the lack of individuality in the object, or to the fact that the European artist—justly or unjustly—is much less convinced of his artistic ability and talent than his Japanese colleague.

Once his attention has been drawn to it, it appears to the observer that the signatures mostly consist of two or three signs, and that these are Chinese signs which apparently point to a Chinese origin for the objects. In spite of this, however, the object is not Chinese.

Up to the present day there has not been published a Japanese-German, Japanese-English or Japanese-French dictionary that is arranged according to Japanese word signs. But even such a dictionary would not be of any use to those seeking this knowledge because there is not available an encyclopedia containing the Chinese root words in sequence, which should not only include the verbs, substantives, particles, etc., but also the most important geographical, mythological and historical names, names of authors and artists, etc. The Japanese artists however make use of most of the Chinese word signs to write their names.

Another difficulty arises with the realization that the Chinese signs can not only have a Chinese but also a Chinese-Japanese and even a pure Japanese pronunciation. For example: the Chinese word shang chang in Chinese-Japanese is pronounced sho and in Japanese masa. Therefore an artist could be named Sho-ichi, Sho-kazu, Masa-kazu or Masa-ichi. But as we shall see an artist can have two, four, six, to eight different names. He can at one time use the Chinese signs, at another time

the Japanese writings Katakana or Hiragana, or
even make use of a certain kind of stenography.

We may thereby conclude that it is necessary to
learn the Chinese and at the same time various
classes of Japanese word signs, if we are trying to
determine the name of the artist, which is the first
step towards investigating the connections of certain Netsukes, schools and styles.

The Japanese writing partly consists of word
writing and partly of syllable writing.   The former is identical with the Chinese in meaning but
not in pronounciation, as the signs always indicate
one idea; the latter is derived from the Chinese language, each sign signifying only one syllable.   The
expression "word writing" in connection with
Chinese writing is not quite correct, because the
single signs stand for more than our words.   The
Chinese signs rather resemble the word roots of
the European langauges that scatter their roots
and branches in all directions.   The Japanese
syllable writing is again divided into two distinct
kinds, namely the Katakana and Hiragana.   For
seventy-three syllables the Katakana writing pro-
vides forty-seven and with the deviations one hundred and eighty-eight signs, while the Hiragana,

which is more or less of an abbreviated italic type writing, has one hundred and forty-five signs. The latter presents special difficulty in that the separating or joining together of the syllables of a word is arbitrary, while it is perfectly permissible to join syllables that do not belong together.

It is a well known fact that all Chinese and Japanese writing is read from the top downward, and that the lines run from right to left. If only the Japanese, after having discovered syllable writing, had thrown aside the Chinese signs, then the Japanese language would not be so difficult to learn. Both the syllable writings are used in most books only as auxiliary signs and as such are used between or to the right of the Chinese signs, and also to mark the pronunciation of proper names. All these writings appear in connection with Netsukes, as well as a whole string of very difficult abbreviations.

The reading of a Japanese name written in Chinese writing, is done in the following manner: first of all it is necessary to distinguish the two hundred and fourteen class and expression signs of the Chinese language, the so-called radicals, and their sequence, from which the Chinese vocabulary

has been arranged.   These signs are often very
similar to one another.   If the sign itself does not
form a part of the radical, we must find out to
which radical it actually belongs.   This is not as
easy as it appears to be.   Then, in accordance with
certain rules you count the strokes which the sign
has outside of those making up the radical, and
look in a Chinese-Japanese dictionary under the
radical, in order to finally locate the sign among the
two thousand three hundred and fifty mostly used,
or the forty thousand more seldom used, or the
forty thousand most seldom used signs, together
with the Japanese translation and pronunciation.
Indeed, you may look in vain amongst the eighty
thousand signs.

In the first place the sign or syllable, as has already been mentioned, can have the most manifold
meanings and pronunciations.   A sign can be
read as follows: sei, sho, uni, ara, ike, iki, oi,
hae, nama, iku, ayaniku, uzu, mana, nari, kizaki,
etc. in accordance with the order of the words and
their connection, or according to whether the word
in question originates from literature, history,
geography, art, theatre, fairy stories, etc.   What
would a person do, if one of his artist friends for

instance placed before him a No album with the
friendly request to read and translate for him the
Japanese-Chinese annotations contained therein?
Would he confess that far from being able to understand half of it, he cannot even read the words?
Our letter writing is easy to learn, and anybody
may be able to read aloud fluently to a Japanese a
book on mathematics without himself understanding any of its contents.   This is not the case with
Chinese-Japanese.   The word signs, expression
signs and syllable signs have a different expression
and meaning, when they are used in connection
with different sciences, and in such cases can only
be read when they are understood and visa versa.
They may perhaps be compared with our scientific
abbreviations and our technical trade expressions.
For instance, with us the latin letter R. on a map
of Canada stands for river, in a work of botany it
may mean ranunculus.   While a university man
can deduce that the word "cinquecento" has something to do with the number five hundred, he will
not be able to explain, even though he may have
a knowledge of art history, how it is that this word
is to be interpreted as the renaissance of the 16th
century A. D.   "Madonna Sistina" is, not for the

artistic mind, but for the philological mind an entirely enigmatical expression.

In our world, abbreviations like the afore-mentioned "R" are mostly limited to special works or maps of foreign countries; it cannot be expected that the greater masses of educated people understand them; "Cinquecento" and "Madonna Sistina" only count for those people who have been educated in the history of art. Words written the same way and having the same pronunciation, but with a different meaning, and words with the same spelling but with a different pronunciation and different meaning, exist in our vocabulary and as in the Japanese language, they are the subject of jokes, picture puzzles, etc. An example of the first class is as follows: (German) Reif = ring, Reif = hoar-frost, reif = the opposite of not ripe; and an example of the second class is the following: (German) der Dachs (meaning an animal, nominative case, des Dachs (genitive of das Dachs) (Meaning Roof). We could not tell the Japanese what the meaning of Reif and Dachs is, when these and similar words are presented for translation into Japanese, without there being anything to indicate in what sense they are to be used. While the words with a double sense in the European languages represent exceptions, we may safely say that they constitute the rule in the Japanese language. As a proof of this, it is sufficient to mention that there are very few root words in the Japanese dictionary that have only one way of spelling, one pronunciation and only one meaning.

Unfortunately the difficulties do not end here. For each syllable may not only be written in Hiragana, Katakana and Chinese-Japanese, but in the last analysis it may be written in many other ways: in ordinary Kaisho printing (three kinds) in Sosho script, italics (three kinds) in Gyosho (round, three kinds) and more seldom in Tensho (Fancy writing for inscriptions and stamps, five kinds) as well as Reisho (Book title writing, many kinds, an abbreviated Tensho), a total of about twenty different kinds of writing.

We may conclude from this that the words sho or masa can be written with four Japanese and twelve Chinese-Japanese signs, and that the twelve Chinese-Japanese signs can be represented by about twenty different kinds, so that it is necessary to know two hundred and forty-four signs in order to be able to read sho or masa alone.

The variety in pronunciation and the very marked deviations which occur sometimes in the different kinds of writing, are shown by the following examples:

Pure Japanese Pronunciation	Japanese-Chinese Pronunciation.	Writing	Writing
KUN:	On		
tomo	yu	Kaisho	Tensho
yoshi	ka	Sosho	Reisho
yatsu	hachi	Reisho	Kaisho
tada	chu	Sosho	Tensho
tatsu	ryu	Sosho	Kaisho
hayashi	rin	Tensho	Reisho
shige	ju	Gyosho	Kaisho

From the word hayashi (woods) you can see how a part of the Chinese expression sign has originated, namely from an image of the object expressed by the word. The sign represents two trees. One

syllable may also have many different meanings.
The syllable min for instance means: people, pearl,
to sleep; the syllable ko or ko: tiger, river, shiny,
hard, red, broad, old, sea, filial devotion, plants,
happiness, high and well born, trade.   If one happened to come across an artist in Europe by the
name of Min-ko, it would be hard to tell whether
it is written Min-ko or Minko, as long as the
Chinese word sign is not given together with the
pronunciation.   Neither can it be ascertained
whether ten Netsukes marked with the name Min-
ko have been produced by two, three, five or ten
artists of that name, or whether they have been
carved by one and the same person; whether the
gentleman in question is named shiny pearl, or
red people, or sleeping tiger, or whether he has formerly borne the three names one after the other.
For artists whose names are composed with the
syllable ryo, ryo or ryu, Brockhous has found sixteen different forms with the following meanings
attached to them: note, price, good, big hill, endure,
pavilion, vice commissioner, edge, silk damask,
dragon, corn, river, prosperity, six, pasture and to
stand.

In writing the Japanese can understand the

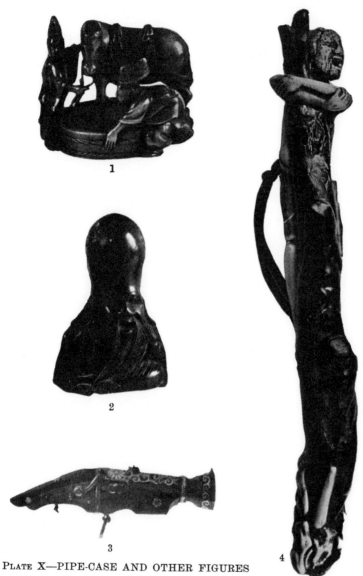

PLATE X—PIPE-CASE AND OTHER FIGURES

1. Men washing horse, (ivory). 2. Fukurokuju, (wood). 3. Flintlock
    gun, (wood and metal). 4. Pipe case, (wood and bone).

Chinese, and visa versa (provided the Japanese
uses the Chinese word arrangement); in speaking
however, this is not the case.   It requires seven
years for a Japanese schoolboy to learn how to
read; the European layman can eliminate all of
this difficulty right from the beginning.   For the
collector, however, nothing remains but to turn for
help to a European sinologist who does not understand the first thing about Japanese art, art handicraft or trade, or call upon a Japanese who must
be an art historian before he is able to do as much
as pronounce the proposed name.   It so happens
that the names of these same Netsuke carvers in
Western literature, can be read Taka-mitsu or
Jo-man, Suke-mitsu or U-man, Nori-zane or Ho-
jitsu, Kazu-tora or I'-ko, whereas they should be
read as being the names of one famous carver
named Min-ko, while there are certainly at least
seven artists with the same *sounding* name, who
write their names in different ways.   In all this
Brockhous has not taken into consideration the
many typographical errors appearing in the European works, nor the fact that many carvers who
were only partly educated or not educated at all,
have been misled by the similarity of sound of the

syllables and have made use of erroneous and partly nonsensical signs to write their names.

It must also be said that many Japanese syllables
are pronounced differently in the Easterly, West-
erly, Northerly and Southerly provinces of Japan.
The same syllable has been transcribed into European books in many different ways, according
to the province from which the Japanese comes
who may be assisting the European with advice,
according to the degree of his philological accuracy
or his literary and artistic education.

The greatest confusion exists in European literature for the reading and writing of names, due
to the fact that the European nations carry out
their own method of transcribing foreign sounds,
and also because no distinction is made in the
printing of the same, between the short and long
syllables such as ho and hō, ko and kō, kyo and kyo
and others, and because the syllables are not given
disjointed.

As previously stated, when Chinese writing is
utilized for the writing of proper names, they can
be read either in Japanese-Chinese or in pure
Japanese.   The Japanese-Chinese pronunciation
which has originated in China, is named On, and

is divided again into Goon, the pronunciation from Southerly China, and Kanon the more elegant pronunciation from Northerly China. The pure Japanese pronunciation is Kun or Yomi. Sometimes the first, at other times the second reading is correct, (example: Shu-zan and not Aki-yama); and when there happens to be a Buddhist pronunciation of the word, as frequently occurs in the divine service, literature and art of Buddhism, the pronunciation corresponding to Goon is correct (ex: Ho-gen and not Ho-gan).

It also happens that the pronunciation of one sign of the name is Japanese-Chinese and the other Japanese, in which case it seems quite probable that both signs of the name are pronounced in Japanese-Chinese or in Japanese. Certain terminations like sai, which appears so often, indicate that the syllables preceding them are to be read in Japanese-Chinese. On the other hand, the names are again pronounced differently, according to whether they represent family names, first names, or artist's names, of all of which the European has no knowledge and which consequently add greatly to the already existing confusion—or according to the unknown pronunciation to which the bearer of the name has given preference.

Although a student of the Japanese language must know something about proper names, Chamberlain advises him not to enter into this too deeply. This is sound for the simple reason that time and effort can be put to a much more profitable use. They are the outgrowth of the Japanese graphic system and frequently an enigma for the Japanese himself. A striking proof of this was offered at the opening of the Japanese Parliament in 1889. One of the first motions adopted mentioned that the names should not be read and pronounced as the bearer of the same had been accustomed to pronounce them heretofore, but after the ordinary Chinese-Japanese pronunciation of the end syllables which form the names. Thus: Mr. Kazu-masa would be named I'-sei, Mr. Tsuyoshi, Mr. Ki. A close study of what the Japanese Parliament disclaims can be best put off by a foreigner to a better time.

If we adopted this plan for our use, we would not make the slightest progress. If we desire to orientate ourselves in the most elementary manner on artists and art schools, we must go a little further into the subject and learn as much about it as is possible for the foreigner to do, just as is done in the following accounts as well as in the list of artist's names and word signs.

The greatest difficulty, not only for the arrangement of names, but also for the identification of the artists themselves, is caused by the large number of names which the Japanese have in general, and the still larger number of names of the Japanese artists in particular.

It is to be pointed out that, like the European, the Japanese names mostly consist of from two to three parts (i.e. Friede-rike, Gott-lieb). Another similarity with Europe consists in that the Japanese have at all times had three names, as the Romans had nomen to designate the race (Tullius), cognomen for the family name (Cicero) and praenomen for the individual (Marcus). To these were occasionally added, as a result of having achieved great acts, or of adoption, etc. a fourth name, agnomen (Africanus, Conctator). Exactly the same thing exists in Japan.

As in Germany where the family names of the nobility have only been in existence since the 12th century, and those of the commoners only since the

14th century, both having been in general use for
the past 300-400 years, while prior to that time the
first name was used, to which sometimes was added
the descent of the bearer, a place other than his
residence (i.e. Wolfram von Eschenbach, Walter
von de Vogelweide, etc.), the name of a property
situated in a certain town or village, or the name
of a castle; so has Japan adopted this custom,
probably during the Taira period, 931-1183.   The
Japanese family name which is not used by the
ordinary classes any more than the clan names,
originally indicated the birth place or residence, as
for instance Yamamoto: "Foot of the mountain."
The first name is not necessarily carried through
one's entire life, but is changed with the greatest
ease at each turning point of a person's life, either
because the individual is adopted, or severs his
adoption—a prevailing Japanese custom—and for
many other reasons.   Places and localities also
change names as for instance: the capital of the
country which was formerly named Yedo, is now
called Tokyo.

The first name, however, is the one which really
characterizes the Japanese artist, as was the custom in Ancient Greece.   Just as in Europe where

a painting of Raphael is identified under that name
and not his family name which is Sanzio, where a
book of Aldus is marked with his first name instead
of Manuzzi, so is the first name of the Japanese
artist used to mark his works, the difference being
that the Japanese artist has two such first names:
a general name (zokumyo, tsusho, yobina) and a
real name (nanori or jitsumyo), which he receives
when he is fifteen years old.   The general names
terminate with taro, oldest son; jiro, second son, or
with yemon, suke, nojo, bei, former official posi-
tions.   The real names like Masashige, Yoshisada,
are only applied on festive occasions together with
the clan names.   The clan name (uji or sei) in all
probability traces its origin back to the assem-
blages of the Yamato tribes who came from the
Southwest and whose successors have produced the
great part of the Japanese population of today.
Uji points to the generical connection. This name
was used exclusively until the increasing power of
the families of the lords of a manor was handed
down to form other branches among the younger
sons who, next to the generical name also had a
special family name.   This clan name was later
given to a Japanese to show that he descended from

a certain ancestor whose religion he was obliged to follow, a rule which continues to hold good under the constitution of February 11, 1889, and also under the new Japanese Civil Code of July 16, 1898. In olden times the clan constituted the whole of the state in which the family was included. After the decline of the clans, the so-called Uji constitution, the family or house took its place in society as it exists today. This explains the synchronic use of the clan—and family names. The four principal clans are: Gen or Minamoto, Hei or Taira, To or Fujiwara, Kitsu or Tachibana. The artists use these clan names, although seldom, for the marking of their art objects.

The artist to be registered under the name Mitsuhide himself wrote his name De-me (family name) Fuji-wara (clan name), Mitsu-hide (first name). To increase the confusion, the Japanese artist, instead of writing the above names on his art productions, eliminates them completely and uses a whole string of other names.

Next comes the child's name (yomyo or osanana), in the place of which is used the real name when the child reaches his fifteenth year. While as a boy he was named Ta-ro or Kiku-no-suke, he is now called Haji-me or Tamotsu. The child's name of the hero Yoshitsune was Ushi-waka.

In addition to this he can, as a grown man, have a surname (if we can call it that), (azana), an elegant name which is supposed to represent Chinese —therefore high—educational development, as for instance, Kun-teki, Bun-rin, Shi-sei (the last name is the azana of the famous historian Sanyo.)

Then follows the artist name, go or gago. The author or artist can, to the great grief of collectors and historians, have several of those names. He can have one name in Tokyo, another in Kyoto, or one as a young man, another one as an elderly man, and a third one as an old man. For instance, To-zan as an old man calls himself To-o. The famous painter Hoku-sai (also a pseudonym or artist name) 1760-1849, son of Nakajima Ise, signs the following names during the course of his life: Shunro (1778-1784), Gummatei (1785), Mugura Shunro (1786-1794), Sori (1795, 1797, 1798), Hokusai (1796 and later). Sori changed into Hokusai (1798-1799), Shinsai (1799), Raito (1800), Kako (about 1804), Hokusai changed into Taito (1816), Taito formerly Hokusai (1817, 1818, 1819), change of Hokusai Taito into Katsuchika

Iitsu (1821), the old fool Iitsu (1824), Manji (1835), Manji the old man foolishly fond of singing (1836 until his death in 1849). On the other hand Katsuchika Taito is the name of one of his pupils. I have given this long list of names according to Goncourt because all of Hokusai's artist names which he used from time to time, can be definitely given. His real name however, is not known. The artist's names often represent local allusions.

It often happens that the artist name can be recognized on the additional syllables like min (people), do (temple, hall), sai (study room), tei (pavilion, summer house), ken (house), ya (house), an (hut), ro (first floor), en, yen, (park), sha (hut), which syllables can be freely changed, so that the same artist can call himself Gyokumin (pearl People), Gyokudo, Gyokusai, Gyokutei, Gyokuken, while it is also possible that a pupil or son or adopted son of Gyokusai, in order to point out this property or to make a distinction between himself and his father or teacher, can call himself, Gyokutei or Gyokuken. It is even known that a teacher, like the painter Toyokuni, has permitted

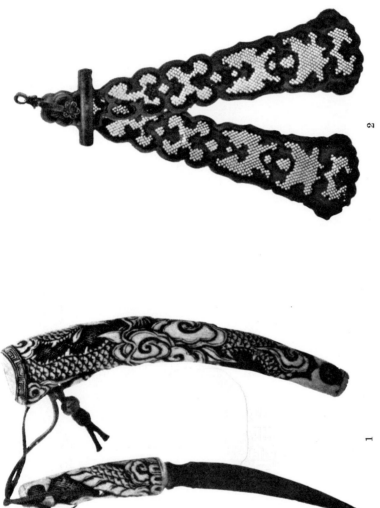

PLATE XI—DAGGER AND INCENSE HOLDER

1. Knife and sheath, (bone and metal).   2. Fan Incense Holder, (ivory).

his pupil to use the same names as himself, in order to facilitate the sale of the art products. The pupil of Hokusai have the following artists names which embody the first half of their teacher's name: Hoku-ba, Hoku-kei (Hok-kei), Hoku-ju, Hoku-un. The second half of the artist name of the master is often utilized in the formation of a new name, so that Toyo-kuni's pupil (Toyo-kuni II) is named Kuni-sada, while the latter's pupil again inherits the second half of the master's name, and is thus called Sada-tora.

A poet signs with a special kind of artist name, a nom de plume which is called haimei, under verses made of seventeen syllables (haikai), i. e. Ki-kaku: an actor, story teller, a geisha, the stage name of geimei, as for instance the actor Dan-ju-ro.

Besides the foregoing real artists names, there is also a kind of additional name, a pseudonym, which is used for special reasons, as for instance in the case of erotic figures and carvings, to conceal the originator. Those names are: Cho-sha, angler; Yu-jin, hermit, priest; Sho-shi, private person; Shy-jin, master, gentleman. These names were written under calligraphy or under verse. There is also the name sei which is used as a mark of respect on the part of the artist in addressing his superiors or his elders.　Therefore: Sei-ryo-do, Gyoku-yen, Yujin, Shun-ko Cho-sha, Ho-rai San-jin; Kio-yen Ko-ji, Kio-yen Sei.

The last is the posthumous namē, homyo or kaimyo, which the Buddhist priest inserts in the obituary notice of every deceased person.　These names end with in, koji, shinji, shinnyo, doji, etc., according to the age, race and religion of the person; for instance the Kaimyo of the famous sword decorator Joi was Kikenin Ryoshu Shinji.　High personnages like the Mikados, on account of their superiority, have a special Shintoistic posthumous name (okurina); the Okurina of the famous Shogun Iyeyaso was To-sho-gu.

To the general name, which is the first name, belongs the name (yobina) a woman's name which when preceded by the syllable O designates honor, like in O Kiku, "lady" or "Lady chrysanthemum," etc.

From this results that we can classify the names in the following categories:

Japanese	English	Example
myoji, uji	family name	De-me
zokumei, zokumyo Tsusho yobina	first name, general name, professional name	Suke-za-ye-mon
nanori, na jitsumei, jitsumyo imina (posthum)	first name from the 15th, cent. on, real first name	Yasu-hisa
uji sei, kabane	clan name	Fuji-wara
yomyo osanana	child's name	Ushi-waka
azana	surname	Shi-sei
go gago	artist name	Hoku-sai
haimei, haimyo geimei	additional name poet's name stage name	San-jin Ki-kaku Dan-ju-ro
homyo kaimyo	posthumous name of the Buddhists	Kikenin Ryoshu Shinji
okurina	posthumous name of high personnages	To-sho-gu

It has not as yet been ascertained which Netsuke carvers made use of some of the above categories.   Perhaps the number of the most important would not be very much reduced if the signature of different names could be proved to be those
of the same person.

If only the artists would use their names in a
way in which they could be identified.   Mutilations
also occur whereby one sign is given, representing
the signature, and this sign can be either the first
or last half of the first name, the artist name or
the family name, like: fuji, gi, ko, koku, mitsu, ren,
setsu, shin, hide, de, etc.   One artist makes a joke
by alluding to the famous De-me (outstanding
eyes) family of mask carvers, when signing with
a name like Me-de O-me, "happy stupid big eye,"
or with Me-de-ta Me "goggle eye"—"happy stupid
eye," names which he composes himself.   Another
artist will sign U-wa-sa, "chattering" on a figure
representing a human being in the act of sneezing,
this with reference to the proverb which says that
"he who sneezes is being chattered about."

The order in which the names of persons, who
use several names at once, are given, is as follows:
artist name (K), family name (F), eventual clan

name (C), first name (V). Like the Hungarians,
the Japanese place their first name after the family name. Judging from the many changes that
occur, it seems that the order in which the names
follow as well as the use of one or many names, is
arbitrary. Below are a few examples of the order
and the number of names.

K.F.C.V.	K.F.V.	F.V.	V.
F.V.K.V.	F.K.V.	F.K.	K.
F.K.V.V.	F.V.K.	K.F.	F.
	F.C.V.		

It is also the custom to use the first syllable of
the family name and of the first name: one syllable
only of the family name, (i.e. De for De-me); only
one syllable of the artist name (i.e. Ko for Ko-ryu-
sai). Thus the carver has the four following
names: Kami-bayashi Gyuka Rakushiken Keimei.
These names represent: a myoji, a tsusho and at
the same time a go, a jitsumei. Or the carver
is named: Okano Shoju Yasunori Heizaburo;
which means that he has a myoji, a go, a jitsumei
and a tsusho.

It is therefore difficult, if not impossible, especially for a person who is not a Japanese, to determine the identity of the carver, or even to pick the

real name from the large collection of the real and
acquired first names, adoptive and pupil names,
artist names and even posthumous names.   The
same first name appears more than once among the
names of the same family, not only as the name
of the father, ·son and grandson (s. Tomo-chika),
but frequently also as the selfchosen petname of all
the sons of a famous or much loved father.

On the other hand, it is not seemly to keep a first
name or an artist name when it has already belonged to a famous artist who is not related to the
family, so that we may suppose that the Netsukes
signed with the name Shu-zan in the same syllable
script, actually have been made by this once famous master.   It may be that one of his pupils has
acquired Shu-zan's name after the latter's death,
as the painter Kunisada bears the name of Toyo-
kuni II, or the pupils of Mi-wa I who are named
Mi-wa II and Mi-wa III.   If such is not the case,
an artist whose first name is Nao-masa, would call
himself Nao-mitsu, Mitsu-sada or any other name
that may seem fit to him, if a famous Nao-masa had
already existed before him.

There is a carver by the name of Tomo-kazu and
also one named Kasu-tomo; the latter apparently

is a pupil of the first named artist. It is even more difficult to imagine that Nori-zane and Ho-jitsu are presumably the same person, and I'-po-sai his pupil. The first two names are different pronunciations of the same script signs, while I-ichi represents a syllable which is added by the pupil, and the syllable nori or ho in this case is pronounced po, the final syllable sai characterizing the name as an artist name. Whether Masa-hisa and Sho-kyu-sai are teacher and pupil or two names for one and the same person, also Masa-tomo and Sho-yu-sai, cannot be determined.

As certain names have been used by artist generations for many centuries, as is the case with Go-to, De-me, Shiba-yama, it must be determined first whether names like the foregoing are family names and as such could belong to several individuals.

Much room is left for investigation as to which artists with the same parts of names or parts of names having the same spelling and pronunciation, have had relations as teacher and pupil. Would there for instance, be a connection between the many artists who have the syllable masa incorporated in their name, and the famous Masa-nao, because they use the same signs for this syllable, or in spite of the fact that they make use of a different sign?

It would be equally interesting to ascertain whether the various artists with the same family name (i.e. O-no, Sei-min, O-no Ryu-raku, O-no Ryu-min) belong together as relatives or as adopted pupils of a famous family.   We find the name of the Myo-chin family from the 12th century until the end of the 19th century (wrought iron work and chased work); the family Go-to during many centuries, etc.

In very few cases, the artist has himself placed on his work further details which would or would not lead to his identification.   The inscription on one Netsuke reads:—"Tomi-haru of Kaaigawa in the province of Iwami has carved this piece at the the age of fifty-seven during the first year of the Kwansei period (1789) in the month of December."   This inscription is only one mm. wide and twenty-seven mm. long! When then was Mr. Tomiharu born? The Japanese counts the birth year and also the current year as a whole year.   For instance, a child born in the afternoon of December 31st, after having been alive for twelve hours, is two years old.   This ancient calculation is called

Kyu-reki, the European kind Shin-reki.   As this
fact is very little known, a great many mistakes
are made in connection with the data on birth years
and ages of Japanese people.   In the case of Tomiharu, the European will be inclined to assume that
he was born in 1732 because he was fifty-seven
years old in 1789, whereas he was only born in 1733.
That this artist was born in 1733 has been con-
firmed by a second Netsuke dated: "1794, sixty-
two years old."   But what is the name of the
artist?   Tomiharu is neither an artist name nor
a family name; presumably it was a first name.
Another Netsuke is signed: "Kiyo tomi haru sei
yo do ka ai gawa iwa mi ten mei otsu shi," consequently this piece was carved in 1785 in Kaaigawa,
or on the river Kaai, in the province of Iwami, by
a man whose artist name was "Seiyodo," or "in
the Seiyo house." He has the family name of Kiyo
or the family name Kiyotomi or a family name a
part of which is Kiyo.   In the first case the he is
a she and is named "Miss Springtime!"   There
is a fourth Netsuke bearing the following inscription: "Carved and certified by stamp of Miss (or
Mrs.) Tomiharu, with Seiyodo as an artist name,
of Kaaigawa, province of Iwami."   Wouldn't this

lady, who still carved when she was sixty-two years old, be happy to know that people concerned themselves about her one hundred and seventy-two years after her birth.

Fixing the dates also presents many difficulties. Either the carver does not give the date with accuracy, or we are confronted with a false inscription. For instance, the inscription on one Netsuke reads as follows: "Ninth year of the Bukwa period, year of the goats." This is inaccurate because the ninth year (1812) of that period was that of the monkeys, and the eighth year (1811) that of the goats.

It seems that giving the age of the artist is only done in cases where, in the eyes of the Japanese, it has reached an astonishing length, or else because the perfection of his work has been very great. Would the ever re-occurring numbers have any particular significance in the life of the persons, as with us the "Anniversary" of the 70th or 80th birthday? A person having grey hair signs, as an old man, o or so. A carver (Gam-bun) places after his name the word rojin "old man;" another one signs only sandai "third generation," the latter probably an artist name.

The pupil relations are also given: "Toshi-take,

pupil of Toshi-haru of Chikuzen." Another one informs us of his imitation of another man's work with the following words: "Kuni-hiro made this after a model of Shu-zan."

The marking: Motome ni ojite or Konomi ni ojite, "upon request," is encountered occasionally and points to an order received from a customer. On one Netsuke is a regular dedication, namely: "A gift to Mr. Shiransai from Haku-yei-sai, who carved this."

It is not astonishing that a carver gives his residence. But what is his idea in giving only the name of the province in which he lived? Very many other interesting marks are found on the Netsukes. Another gives a Chinese verse like: "Spring and Spring Tides have come together." A third one makes the following inscription: "I killed (!) the whale from whose fish bone I have carved this scolopendrid, when at the age of 60 I travelled along the Tokaido." On an erotic Uzume is written: "It happened that in the tenth month of the Boshin year (1788), Minko, subject of the Daimyo of Tsu, carved this piece more or less as a joke." On a crab Netsuke was inscribed the following: "It was during the last ten days of the sixth (summer) month, of the monkey year, the ninth of the Bunkwa period (1811 or 1812) on the Island of Izukushima in the province of Geishu, when I, Yujin "the hermit," my two artists names being Seiryodo and Gyokuyen, carved this crab, who is a dweller in the water, out of a boar's tooth." This inscription placed in three perpendicular parts is altogether two mm. wide and seven cm. long.

A Netsuke representing an archaic saga animal, made of wood painted in different colors bears the inscription "Rare. Possessor Kasho." This signifies that the famous painter Ikeno Taigado, surname Kasho, who lived from 1723-1776, was the owner of this rare piece. If on the other hand the carver Shun-ko-sai declares on the under side of the Netsuke in beautiful well framed script, that the figure represents the devil "Shundendoji," this is not a sign of the grace of God having been bestowed upon the artist.

Many artists place upon their original works a special mark which is used by them alone and which is named Kakihan or Kwao. It means: kaki-to write, to sign; han-stamp, press, press plate; therefore a seal to certify that something has

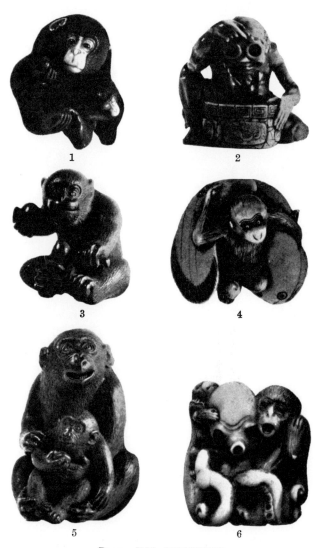

PLATE XII—MONKEYS

1 Monkey, (wood and coral). 2. Monkey looking at coral plant,
(ivory). 3. Monkey eating nut, (wood). 4. Monkey and
fish, (ivory) 5. Monkey and baby, (wood).
6. Monkey and Octopus, (wood).

been written, signed and printed. The Kakihan of an artist may in some way be connected with one of the signs or with the first and second sign of his name, and as a rule not with the family name or artist name, but with the first name. It happens sometimes that an apparently well known artist places his Kakihan on a Netsuke without adding his name, in which case it is necessary to know the mark before one is able to identify the maker of the object. There are also artists who write their name in the same way and use a Kakihan that has one stroke more or less than another, but is otherwise the same, this designating that the respective artists are members of one and the same family or school. It seems that the Kakihan also proves the genuineness of the carving like the Saiku-in stamp (literally "trade mark") which appeared on so many works, and which, according to Yokoi has not been used since De-me Do-haku (1633-1715.)

Other significant signs with which certain Netsukes are marked, are those that represent titles granted by the Mikado. No artist who carved only Netsukes has received such a title. The first three of the following titles were mostly given to physicians, painters (especially those of the Kano school) or sculptors, (and on rare occasions to sword decorators, as for instance: Goto Ichijo:)

Hokkyo: Hogen: Hoin: Tenkaichi.

The Hokkyo which is the title of a Buddhist order, seems to be the lowest in rank. Ryu-kei, and Sessai are two Netsuke carvers who had this title. The next higher is the Hogen, also a Buddhist title, which was given to De-me Hiro-aki, Kiku-tei, Raku-min, Ran-tei, Sessai, Shu-getsu, Shu-zan. The painter Kano Motonobu (1477-1559) was named Ko-Hogen, "the old Hogen." The next is Hoin, which is the highest honor title. Brockhous does not know of any Netsuke carver who acquired this title. According to Anderson, the order in which the titles follow is just the reverse. The highest title conferred by the Shogun, and which is born especially by mask carvers and manufacturers of metal mirrors, but not by painters or Netsuke carvers as such, is the Ten-ka-ichi title.

Should we refrain from making a study of these things and be guided only by the conclusions of the experts, our labors would be in vain. There are a

few noteworthy carvers of Japan, but in view of
the fact that the names of these artists are syste-
matically forged, their analysis is of very little
importance in the estimation of the age or artistic
value of a Netsuke.

CHAPTER VII

THE priesthood, church arrangements, and utensils pertaining to the divine service of the two Japanese religions have been taken as subjects of Netsukes and so have the mythological legends of the people, which are related to these religions.

What the original primitive religion of the Japanese was cannot be determined, because the descent of the present inhabitants of Dai Nippon has not yet been determined. The first inhabitants supposedly were cave dwarfs named Koropoku-guru in the language of the Ainus who supplanted them. Certain people identify them with the Ainus; others claim that they were their predecessors. The Japanese called the Ainus Yezo or Yebisu, barbarians. They were driven to the North by the Yamato tribe who entered Japan through the Southwest, into Kyushu, on or about 660 B. C. This Yamato tribe was supposedly composed of the immediate successors of an Amaterasu ancestress.   Those belonging to the higher classes, the so-called nobility type, Daimyogao, are much taller, with a fine Chinese oval-shaped face, while the remainder of the present day Japanese are small, round-faced Mongol-Malayans with very pronounced jaws and often slit eyes.   We very seldom find Polynesian blood, or descendants of Kanakas or Negritos.   On account of the mixture of races big round eyes are also found which point to Aryan (?) or Malayan descent.   Ainus as well as Indians and Hollanders, and the Indian Saga figures were made by the Netsuke carvers, with Aryan eyes.

Besides Christianity, Japan has two religions, Shintoism and Buddhism.   Not only does a part of the population practise either one or the other religion, but the majority of the people worship the Gods of the one as well as of the other.   The protection of a Shintoist God is besought for a Japanese upon his birth, while the death celebration is performed in accordance with the rites of the Buddhist sect to which the family of the deceased belongs.   The original universal religion of the Yamato tribes was a cult of ancestors and heroes, which is similar to the primitive religions of most

people.   At first heaven, the seat of the Gods, was
identified with this religion.   The celestial bodies,
the sun and the moon, the elements and the powers
of nature were worshipped.   The sun was greatly
worshipped.   Also the souls of dead people of
great merit were worshipped under the name of
powerful, invisible spirits, Kami.   There even
exist deified forebears of a whole community as
well as of separate families.   The origin of the
founder of the present dynasty Jimmu Tenno (660
B. C.) was traced back to the God of the sun
Amaterasu, and many Kamis were named.   To
these were added a great many devils and demi-
gods standing between Creatures and Gods.

The Shintoist temples neither have statues nor
images, because the Shintoists believe in invisible
Gods.   In the sanctuary, which is made by means
of a curtain, are only found a highly polished metal
mirror and a bundle of white paper strips attached
to a staff, both being probably symbols of clean-
liness of soul and body, and of an irreproachable
life, as prescribed by Shintoism.   In the temple of
Atsuta is seen the sword of the Susanoo which re-
calls the delivery of the world from a terrible
dragon. The Goheis originally were dusters which,

during prayer were used as a symbol of the deity itself and also served to keep the dust out of the atmosphere. The celebrating of the official ceremony for the worshipping of ancestors as superhuman beings was not only the duty of the individuals but also that of the foremost head of the race. The worshipping of the first Goddess Amaterasu was the duty of the emperor alone, a duty which was transferred to the latter's representatives in the provinces. The duties of the clergy were limited to the teaching of religious and moral laws, delivering sermons and the execution of songs and holy dances which accompanied certain ceremonies. The priests are allowed to marry, and today distinguish themselves from other people only by the dress they wear during divine service. From 1868 until 1878 Shintoism was the national Japanese state religion which caused the influence of the 1300 year old foreign Buddhism to decline. Shintoism has done away with its religious nature and is now considered solely as a forefathers' cult. Ever since that time the higher classes, the nobles and their families have their obituary ceremonies performed in accordance with Shintoist rites, and those of the lower classes are performed as they were before, in accordance with Buddhist rites.

In the beginning was chaos. Then a number of Gods were created, and later again Izanagi and Izanami, brother and sister, came into existence, and condensed the chaotic world to countries and seas. From Izanagi's limbs and clothes were formed new Gods, among whom Amaterasu, the goddess of the sun, her brother the god of the moon, and finally, out of Izanagi's nose, the wild god of storm, Susanoo. Susanoo has for his domain the nether world and the sea, and Amaterasu the upper world. An offense by her brother caused her to retire to a cave, so that the sun shone no longer. The goddess Uzume, through cunning and comic dances persuaded Amaterasu to reappear, and thereby is credited with having given the sun back to the world. Later Amaterasu sent her grandson Ninigi to earth to reign over Japan, and gave him the holy mirror, a sword and a jewel, the symbols of a pure soul, of courage and of wisdom. He in turn handed them down to his great-grand-son, the first emperor Jimmu (660 B. C.), and from that time on they have been considered the most precious treasures of the Mikado. Through

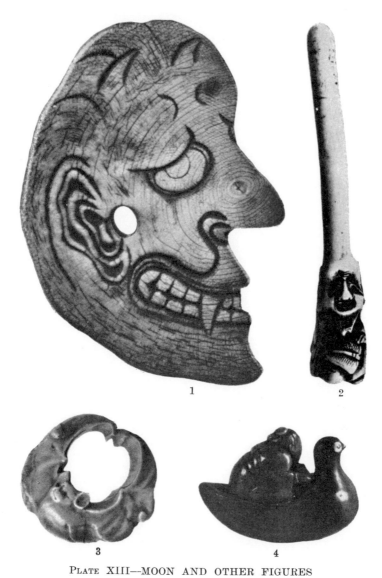

PLATE XIII—MOON AND OTHER FIGURES

1. Moon, (ivory). 2. Fukurokuju, (bone). 3. Bat, (ivory). 4. Woman
and pigeon, (wood and ivory).

Jimmu the emperors of Japan, down to the present reigning Mikado, are descendants in a direct line from the goddess of the sun.

All kinds of animals are taken care of in the temples of some gods: stags, pigeons, herons, ravens, tortoises, carp, foxes, which are taken for a kind of God-like messenger. These animals are not worshipped as the ibis, the crocodile, the ichneumon, the cat and steer were worshipped by the Egyptians.

The cult consists principally of the temple feasts, of ceremonies, Harai, through which the priests purify the souls of the living, and of prayers, Inori, with which they implore the help of God. They believe in the immortality of the soul, but have only a vague idea as to the after world.

For many centuries the clever Buddhist priests adapted their doctrine and the manifestations of Buddha to Shintoism, to such an extent that almost all the Gods seem to belong to the one as well as to the other religion, each one having several corresponding names. The heaven gods, are not at all or very rarely reproduced in art, whereas the happy Uzume frequently appears in the form of Netsukes.

At the end of the third century A. D. the
Chinese philosophical doctrines of Confucius were
introduced through the Korean Wani (holy
books), and with them the writing, the language
and culture of the Chinese people. In the same way
the heavenly, earthly and human gods of Taoism
reached Japan.   Gods and goddesses of wind,
thunder, seas, fire, sustenance and illness, of mountains and water, rivers, temples and trees, were
worshipped—about eight million gods in all.   All
his gods, Shintoist, Taoist, Buddhist, if represented at all by the Japanese artist, are treated
with a familiarity and a delightful humor, which
it is difficult for the Western people to reconcile
with worship and honor.   Even among Christian
people, however, punishments have been imposed
upon ungracious or ineffective deities, and earthly
beings are spoken of as "holy" by other earthly
beings, which indicates a certain amount of inti-
macy between those who are praying and those who
are being prayed to.

As far as the representation of Shintoist and
Chinese gods is concerned, it resembles the art of
the Buddhist transcendant figures.   Raiden, the
god of thunder, and Oni the little Buddhist devil,

have horns and claws, Uzume and the Buddhist priest Daruma might be taken for brother and sister. The amalgamation of form is naturally based upon an amalgamation of the conceptions of the god which plays a great part in the religious belief of the Japanese people.

Uzume, mostly named Okame, the Shintoist goddess, who, through her dance has invited the goddess of the sun, Amaterasu, to come back out of the cave to which she had retired after having been offended by her brother, Susanoo, the god of the storm is represented as a corpulent female figure with heavy puffed cheeks, smiling face and generally with two black spots on the forehead representing painted eyebrows.

Between the real Japanese Shintoist god figures and those of the Buddhist type, which were only introduced in the 6th century A. D., there appears a sort of connecting link in the seven gods of fortune, which were found in every Japanese household. They were greatly worshipped and summoned to exercise their power in favor of those believing in them. They are original Shintoist (Japanese), Taoist (Chinese), Brahmanic (Indian) and Buddhist (Indian) gods, who are transfigured both inwardly and outwardly. Their special functions toward the deserving people are: precautions for a long life and wisdom,—Fukurokuju; wealth and comfort,—Daikoku; daily exigencies,—Ebisu; happiness,—Hotei; good luck in war,—Bishamon, of whom Brockhous has never seen a Netsuke; scientific fame,—Jurojin; knowledge and wealth, Benten.   To these are occasionally added Inari (the God of rice, fox) and the Japanese gods of fortune Kasuga and Itsukushima, the Shintoist gods Sarudahiko (red face, long red nose, and mate of Uzume), Okuninushi, Koyane and Sukunahikona.

Fukurokuju, God of Fortune, whose name is "wealth — happiness — longevity," comes from China and may probably be identified with Lao-tse therefore of Taoist origin, is represented by an old man with a long, white beard, clad in a philosopher's costume, with an enormously elongated skull, which had developed to that extent by his hard thinking as to how he can make people happy. Next to him are often found tortoises, cranes or stags, in the hand a carved staff, paper roll or jewel.

Ebisu or Yebisu, pronounced Ebis, supposedly

is of Shintoistic origin, the third son of the creators of the world Izanagi and Izanami, who, at the age of three was not able to walk and was therefore disowned by his parents, sent forth in a boat and left to his own fate. He was named Hiruko. In contrast to the other gods of fortune he is represented in Japanese court attire, with a peculiar bonnet, usually with a fish, such as bream, tai, or an angle.

Hotei, literally meaning "bag of cloth" is the half Taoist and half Buddhist god of fortune who appears more frequently than any other. He is more of a fat, happy "old boy" than a creature worthy of being worshipped. He has a great preference for children and is mostly represented with a big bag over his shoulders, which contains the takaramono, the costly treasure of Buddhism, and always with the lower part of his body naked. A shaved head points to the fact that he was a priest originally. He is supposed to be a caricature of the Maitreya Buddha.

Daikoku, which means "big black man" is identical with the Buddhist Mahakala. Even though represented in Chinese civilian or court attire with peculiar head dress he is of pure Japanese origin. He carries a hammer and attempts to carry also a

bag containing the Takaramono on his shoulder, or
to stand on two rice bales.   The rat is often associated with him as a symbol of rapid increase, hence
wealth.   The hammer serves the purpose of incor-
porating the In and Yo (the male and female principle) and so leads to the evolution of all things.

Jurojin, in the Japanese representation easily
mistaken for Fukurokuju, is another conception of
the same god.   Like Fukurokuju he often appears
accompanied by cranes, white stags or tortoises,
but wears a transparent cap, which identifies him.
He is represented as an earnest, upright man,
worthy of being worshipped, in the attire of a
Chinese sage.

Benten, the only representative of the beautiful
sex among the seven gods of fortune, is of Brahmanic and therefore of Indian origin, and presumably identical with Sarasvati, the wife of Brahma.
She is represented as a beautiful woman with a
crown, occasionally with a musical instrument as a
symbol of harmony, often with a dragon, a serpent
or seated on a mythical animal.

While the Shintoist worshipping of forefathers
had been the duty of a very few people, the Buddhist religion brought other ideas into the country,

namely the doctrine of a supreme creature ruling over all other beings, the duty of everyone to worship it and emulate its sanctity. On the other hand, not only the responsible race leaders, but also every individual could look forward to living forever in the next world as a god-like creature, in accordance with his or her good or bad earthly deeds.

Buddha, in Japanese Butsu, whose real name was Siddhattha, of the wealthy and noble race of the Sakyo, a branch of which is named Gotama, lived in the 6th century B. C., was born in India, and died when he was eighty years old, in 480 B. C. His doctrine: of suffering, of the origin of suffering, of elevation from suffering, and of the way to elevation from the same, spread gradually over all Asia. Upon the occasion of the third council held under the reign of King Açoka, it was decided to send out missionaries who in 225 B. C. converted first the hinterland of India, and then Ceylon, where the doctrine is practised in its purest form to this day, while in the North it has been changed, and in India has completely fallen into oblivion. At the birth of Christ, Buddhism was introduced into China, and in the 4th century A. D. it was adopted there as the State religion.   In 552 A. D., about one thousand years after Buddhism came into existence, it was brought to Japan from Korea, together with the Chinese writing, where it remained the principal religion until the year 1868, when the old Japanese Shintoist religion, for political reasons, was declared the State religion. Even today, the Japanese recognize both religions, visit their temples and when in distress turn to the gods of the one as well as of the other.   Through his residence the Japanese belongs to the diocese of the Shintoist guardian spirit of the place, to whose care and protection he is entrusted after his birth, but through his descent, through the family, he belongs to the Buddhist sect of the country.   There are twelve Buddhist sects which distinguish themselves primarily by their more or less profound perception of the Buddhist metaphysics and philosophy, through myth and form, and the belief in the power of mysterious signs and forms, as well in their learning as to the various ways by which to reach the Buddhist Heaven, Nirvana, the paradise of the West, gokuraku.

The "sect of virtue," Zenshu, for instance teaches that meditation, reflection, self-absorption and the truth acquired thereby, leads to one's aims and not the study of holy writings, nor words and deeds. Every Japanese child knows the very popular figure of the proposed author of this creed, The Daruma, a personification of the Buddhist laws, and can tell of him that he spent nine years in a temple, motionless, with his face turned to the wall, absorbed in meditation.

While the original doctrine of Buddha knew only one way for people to redeem themselves, and this was by their own strength, with no mediator between gods and mortals, there came into existence, in the 3rd century B. C., at the time when Buddhism penetrated the great masses of Indian people, a cult, an image service, which soon became a permanent institution of the Buddhist church. The author of this religion and his sixteen or five hundred celebrated pupils were figuratively worshipped as saints. Under the influence of foreign religions which did not attempt to fight Buddhism, but which, on the contrary, adopted it, there came into being a Pantheon with millions of Buddha figures. According to the Mahayana doctrine, which is the northerly form of Buddhism, the creator of heaven and earth, the first Buddha, produced five meditative Buddhas, Dhyani Buddhas, among whom was Amitabha, who, as Amida in Japan, has pushed into the background Gotama, the author of the religion.   The Dhyani Buddhas appear after each other, in our world, as five Manushi-Buddhas, human Buddhas, Amitaba appearing as Gotama; and they have five spiritual sons, the Dhyani-Bodhisatvas, Amitabha den Padmapani, who, transformed into a woman, is greatly honored in China as Kwanyin, in Japan as Kwannon, the goddess of pardon and mercy, as Madonna, (but never as a mother).   The Amida-Dogma, based upon the personification of endless light, as the name indicates, came into existence in Kashmir during the 2d century A. D.

It is the popular belief that Amida thrones on a lotus flower in the "Paradise of the West," where everyone is free from suffering, surrounded by wonderful scenery, beautiful trees, ponds and lotus flowers, and pavilions made of precious stones, and where Amida's glory and praise is sung.

The counterpart of heaven is hell, which was originally a Brahmanic idea. It is placed under the authority of King Yemma, together with many devils, and is subdivided into different parts in

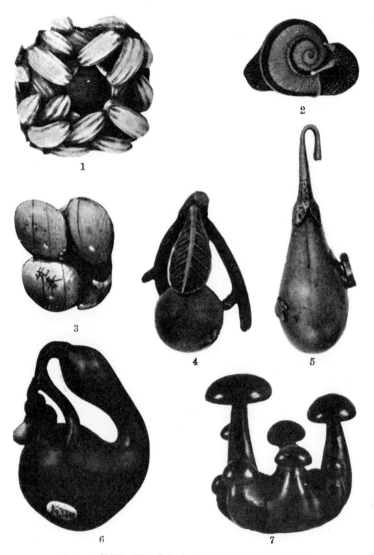

PLATE XIV—VEGETABLES AND FLOWERS

1. Chrysanthemum, (ivory). 2. Snail, (ivory). 3. Nuts, (ivory). 4. Peach, (ivory). 5. Gourd water bottle, (metal). 6. Gourd (wood). 7. Mushrooms, (wood).

which regeneration is made possible after painful purgatory.

From the Brahmanic gods Indra as Teishaku Ten, and Brahma as Bon Ten, have been taken into Japanese Buddhism, under the name of "the two kings" Ni-o. They guard the temple against evil spirits, and their statues are often placed in the outer niche at the entrance of the temple, and are usually of enormous size with a very wicked expression.

Kwannon, Chinese Kwanyin, goddess of mercy and charity, is the most popular of all Buddhist gods. According to the Chinese legend she was the daughter of a king of the Chow Dynasty (696 B. C.) and only later identified with the Indian god Avalokitesvara. She refused a marriage to which her royal father forced her, and was therefore condemned to death. But the sword of the executioner broke without wounding her. Her soul reached hell, but hell, through her presence, was transformed into a paradise, so that the king of hell was forced to send her back to earth. Thus, by miracle, she landed on a lotus flower in the island of Pu-tu.

It appears that in a prize fight with Mata no

Goro, Kawazu won by bringing one of his legs under the knee of his adversary in such a way that the latter fell; Kawazu got on top of him and thereby won the match.   Ever since that time this trick has been called the Kawazu throw.   Kawazu however was shot with an arrow by Kudo Suketsune for which the former's son took revenge on the murderer who was a friend of Mata no Goro, this resulting in a long feud.

The sixteen Rakans, adherents of Buddha, can often be distinguished from the Sennins by the right shoulder and breast which are uncovered, earrings which are worn occasionally, and in pictures, by their halo.   The representation of Rakans and of many Sennins is so uncertain and so seldom recognizable by any characteristic marks it is often difficult to identify the individual personification.

Gama Sennin.   Little is known about this frequently represented person.   The name signifies toad.   He appears to have lived in the mountains, and at one time taken pity on a sick frog or four-legged or three-legged toad.   This animal, in reality was a very wise demon, who, in order to show his appreciation to his benefactor, taught him all kinds of secrets.

The Sennin are celestial beings of Taoist, rarely of Buddhist-Indian, and in exceptional cases, of pure Japanese origin. There are five classes. (1) Doomed geniuses without bodies; (2) geniuses of human nature, who have renounced all physical desires, hermits; (3) earthly geniuses, people who have become immortal on earth, and who live in caves; (4) God-like geniuses, who live in heaven in an incorporeal state, and finally, (5) heavenly gods who have attained the highest purity and perpetual life. The second and third class of these are reproduced in the form of Netsukes. Among them are the eight Taoist Sennins (Shoriken, Tsugen, Ryodohin, Sokokukiu, Tekkai, Kanshoshi, Ransaikwa, Kasenko), which are characterized by a leaf apron pointing to Indian origin, and sometimes also by a leaf collar, uncovered head and heavy hairlocks or braids.

Tsugen is one of the "eight Rishi" of the Taoists and lived towards the end of the 7th century A. D. as a famous nomadic magician. His companion was a white horse which carried him thousands of miles in one day, but which, during the resting periods could be folded together and packed away in his gourd bottle. As soon as he required the services of the horse again, he squirted water on the bottle with his mouth, upon which the animal appeared again in its natural form. He became immortal in 740. Tsugen, the wonderful gourd bottle, and the pliable horse are frequently taken as subjects for art productions.

The gourd bottle supposedly is a sign of the state of celibacy of the Buddhist priest; it is used to moisten the mouth in the morning, which is the period during which the priest may neither eat nor drink.

In the year 110 B. C. the Fairy Queen, Si Wang Mu, left her palace in the Kuen Lun mountains, where the peach tree of the fairies grows,—the fruit of which grants immortality,—to make another visit to her beloved emperor. She took with her seven peaches, of which she ate two in the presence of the emperor Wu Ti. While the latter expressed the desire to keep the stones, she saw through a window Tobosaku: "This child has stolen three of my peaches," she exclaimed, "and is therefore nine thousand years old." He acquired thereby godly wisdom, and became a good advisor to his emperor. He is also represented with the long head of Fukurokuju.

Tekkai is one of the most beloved Taoist Rishis, a pupil of Laotse, and possessed the ability of temporarily separating his soul from his body. Once, when the soul went to visit his teacher in the land of immortals, Tekkai in the meantime asked one of his pupils to take care of his body during his absence, stating that he would return in seven days. On the sixth day the pupil learnt that his mother was ill and ran to her aid, because filial duty came before the duty as a pupil. When Tekkai returned the next day, the body had disappeared and he was compelled to live in a dead toad. Since that time he has a hideous face and is lame.

Bashiko lived during the reign of the Chinese emperor Hwang Ti (2697-2597, B. C.) and was known as a famous veterinarian. Once there appeared before him a dragon, whose cast down ears and open muzzle showed that he was ill. He carried him into his hut and cured him by blood-letting and with licorice, and the dragon, to show his appreciation, carried Bashiko forth on his back to the skies of immortals.

Chinnan also cured people and animals by means

of magic pills.   Despite his supernatural powers, he lived on dog's flesh, dressed in rags, was drunk for days at the time, and won his livelihood by weaving sieves and baskets.   Once he molested the long wished for rain dragon, in the 13th century, and was carried away by the inundation which was brought about, after having lived 1350 years.

Kinko, a Northern Chinese sage, lived around the 12th century.   For two hundred years he taught in the province of Chili and finally drowned himself in a river, with a promise to his pupils that he would return some day.   While ten thousand pupils were awaiting him he appeared on the waves riding on a carp, remained with them another month, teaching, and disappeared once more in water and was never seen again.

The Onis originally were Yakshas, a kind of demon over whom reigned Kubera, one of the four kings of heaven, or guardians of the four heaven directions.   As Bishamon, this Kubera is counted among the seven gods of forune.   Brockhous who has studied the development of the Oni representation from the Buddhist statuary of the 7-12th century, finds that, as long as the Chinese and Korean influence prevailed, the Onis on which the Shitennos stand, do not in any way show signs of pain or torture and are not made with feet. On the contrary, they bear a very happy expression on their face, and willingly offer their back so that their masters may stand on them. As the independence of the Japanese increased, (this already at the end of the 8th century), the facial expression and position of the Onis become more grotesque. The Shitennos step on their face, stomach, etc., and they double up from the suffering thus inflicted upon them. Obviously the meaning of the Oni as a simple inferior, has been misunderstood, and has been taken for a conquered enemy and a bad spirit. Originally the Onis had nothing to do with the principle of evil spirits and consequently there exists no inter-relation between them and our devil or Satan. This is proven by their large number and the laughable, submissive parts which they played. There is nothing in their portrayal of the haughty sovereign of evil who is on the same level with God.

The Buddhist devils, who have been reproduced with a most terrifying expression through the fantasy of the priests, are very seldom represented in the form of Netsukes. On the other hand, the armless, jeering, irritating little devils (Plates VI, 3; VII, 3), such as the people imagine them to be, appear very often, more or less as counterparts of the gods of fortune. With a square head, long straight hair, mostly with two little stumps of horns, in the muzzle two upper and two lower teeth similar to those of a beast, while the others are those of a human being, generally with a very human expression of an Aryan type, in a constrained posture with human muscles, from three to four claws and from two to three toes, with a tiger skin or occasionally a hip-cloth, able to transform themselves into lovable creatures, always ready to play tricks, they closely resemble their Western brothers, the little devils of the fables.

The European represents the devil in black, the negro in white and the Japanese in red. Who is right? Neither one of them has seen him, but each one gives him attributes which make him repugnant. The similarity between the outward form of the Asiatic devil and that of the European, is a subject for thought. Horns, claws, occasionally the cloven hoof, are present in both cases. The classic Gorgon and Medusa, the "wrathful gods" of Lamaism, the Tantra divinities, and a number of similar representations, are in so many respects alike in form, that it is not worth the trouble to make a thorough investigation of this subject. If it was formerly admitted that India was the home of the devil, from which he spread East and Westward, there is more reason to believe today that Northwestern Asia is his home. As according to Darwin, our forefathers had large corner teeth like the anthropoid apes, and used them as dangerous weapons, it is possible that the natural history of the devils coincides with the beginning of the human race. Not only the fangs and the strong flat muscles, but also the third eye on the forehead, which is found occasionally in the Oni are of anthropological interest, since the discoveries of de Graaf and Spencer make it apparent that all the vertebrated animals in prehistoric times, had a third single eye in the middle of their forehead, which rudimentary organ is still present in the pineal gland.

The governor of the Japanese Onis is Shoki, of whom the Onis are very much afraid when he pursues them with a sword, but on whom they play all kinds of tricks. On Sylvester night, dried beans are thrown about in the house, while crying ''Away with the devil, let happiness come in," to chase the devils away.

Daruma, the 28th Indian and the 1st Chinese Buddhist patriarch, the son of a South-Indian king, settled in China in the year 520 A. D. and for nine years remained seated motionless in a temple, absorbed in meditation, after which time his arms and legs, on account of not having been in use, rotted and fell from his body. He is therefore frequently represented as an unshaved head placed on a round body. Standing on reed leaves, he is said to have sailed to Japan, learned Buddhism with good results and died in the Kataoka mountains in the year 613 A. D. He is the originator of the Buddhist sect known as Zenshu.

The Tokko is a symbol in three forms: with one arm, symbolizing the spoke of the wheel of justice, called rimbo; with three arms, called sanko; with five arms, goko. It symbolizes the irresistible power of prayer, of absorption in the belief and of ecstacy. It is said that it was originally meant to represent a diamond sceptre which is carried by priests and magicians.

As their Aryan appearance shows, the mythological creatures: Ashinaga, Tenaga, Shojo,

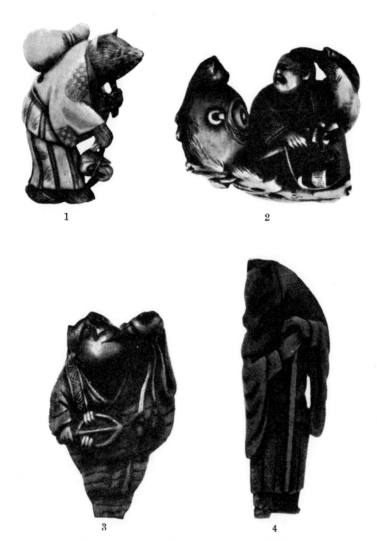

1   2

3   4

PLATE XV—MYTHOLOGICAL FIGURES

1. Badger, (ivory).   2. Man and badger-teapot, (ivory).   3. Man blow-
ing horn, (wood).   4. Fox, (ivory).

Ningyo, ghosts, dwarfs and angels, have this in common, that they appear to descend from the Indian saga. Like other saga figures they have been brought from Korea to Japan via China.

The Ashinagas or long-legged people, and the Tenagas, or long-armed people, are creatures who lived in the North of Manchuria, according to San-hai-king. The legs are over thirty feet and the arms over twenty feet long. The Ashinagas take the Tenagas on their back and carry them into deep water where the long-arms catch a fish with each hand. The long-legs wear their hair hanging down their back. Others thought that they lived in the North of China, "in proximity to the Hung Sheung tree," and according to a third opinion, they lived in the "East of Chi'hshui." Their nudity points to a warm country. In Japanese art they are often represented as allegorical of co-operative work.

The Shojos are mythical creatures of Chinese origin, but completely transferred into the Japanese saga. They live on the sea-coast and the fishermen catch them by means of cups filled with wine. Their red hair and blood is used to extract a dye which is very highly prized by Western people.   It is said that they resemble monkeys (the Orang-Utang is named Shojo), but that they have a face, voice and speech like children.   The proverb says "as drunk as a Shojo."

Ningyo, or human fish, (in our language, mermaid, nix, siren) are mythological creatures.   In India the Matsyanari, mostly of the female sex, pass for the incarnations of the Vishnu, who saved the father of the human race from the flood in the form of a man with a fishtail.   It is said that in Japan the race descends from the land of Taiyan, and the secrets of the deep sea have been gathered from the roaring of the shells.   The goddess Benten also has mermaids for daughters.   According to more recent investigations, the legend once originated through the observation of the Dugong whose mate holds her young, while nursing, with her breast fin.   In Japanese art they are always represented as of Aryan type reigning over ebb and flood, with a round or pointed jewel provided with rings in their arms which guarantees longevity. They are also often represented suckling their young.

In Japan the dwarfs are twenty-five cm. high,

and travel in files and not like worms, so as not to be picked up by their deadly enemies, the cranes.

The saga world of all people has in it mythological animals with supernatural properties. Among those included in the Japanese legends, only the weasel who cuts the sandal straps and scratches the face of the wanderer, the racoon dog, the kappa and the nuye are of pure Japanese origin. Those who come from China are the tortoise, and the sea-turtle with only one eye on her breast plate. Of Indo-Chinese origin are apparently the natural animals who are endowed with supernatural powers, such as: the tiger as a king of the mountain animals, fox, hare, tortoise, heron, wolf (the thunder dog), then the natural animals represented with enormous dimensions; the centipede, the field spider, carps, snakes and monkeys. Some of these are represented with an increased number of limbs, snakes with two heads, a swine with two heads, a monkey with four ears, a fox with nine tails, a fish with one head and ten bodies, and finally the compound monsters, the dragon, the kirin, the baku, the phoenix, the fish with a dog's head and the griffin, the latter partly animal and partly human.

The racoon dog, living in Amur and in Japan, sleeping through the entire winter like the fox is endowed, by the Japanese legends, with all sorts of supernatural craft, as for instance, the ability to change its appearance. Sometimes it resembles more the bear, sometimes more the fox, but always has a fox-tail. It has an enormously extended stomach on which it drums with the paws in order to mislead the wanderer into a swamp.

The Kappa, literally "boy of the river," is a fantastic animal, mostly depicted with a body resembling that of a tortoise, frog legs and a monkey-like head, on the top of which is a hollow which is filled with his watery elixir of life. This creation, nevertheless, is "scientifically" described as a froggy creature, four feet nine inches in height and in 1830 was still caught in swamps. He is in love, is dangerous to young ladies, has a fighting spirit, but is as ceremonious as a nobleman. Before engaging in a duel with a Kappa, man is advised to request that the Kappa make a polite bow. The Kappa, is such a gentleman that he will comply with the request of his adversary but this causes the life giving water to flow out of the hollow on his head so that he is easily conquered.

The Nuye, the noctural bird of legend is a creature with a human body, the legs of a tiger, the head of a monkey, and a tail of a snake with a head on the end. People would never have known about it, had not the noble hero, Minamoto no Yorimasa, in the fourth month of the year 1153 A. D. discovered the Nuye.

There is enough material to write a book on the origin of the dragon myths, their migration from one country to another, about their characteristics and their transfiguration. For the dragon seems to be a reminiscence of the entire humanity of the tertiary period and the worst enemy of the younger human race. In the system of Chinese natural history, four different kinds are distinguished: heavenly dragons, who guard the gods; spiritual dragons, who cause rain and wind; earthly dragons, who create rivers and brooks; and finally the subterranean dragons who safeguard hidden treasures. In addition to these, there is a fifth one of Japanese creation, namely the dragon of the seas. In China and in Japan, the dragon is not looked upon as an evil creature. He can make himself invisible or appear under a different form. The Chinese-Japanese form of the dragon has remained the same for the last two thousand six hundred years: a camel's head, stag horns, devil eyes, ox ears, body similar to that of a snake, scales of a carp and claws of an eagle. Flames gush from his body through the shoulders and hips.

The Kirin has the body and head of a stag with a soft horn which is bent backwards, the tail of a lion, or the head of a dragon provided with the same soft horn, the body of a crocodile. The back part of his body resembles that of a lion with a bushy, curly tail and legs of a stag. He is the noblest animal of the creation and the emblem of extreme kindness. His appearance is a good sign. In Buddhist writing it is stated that he walks so softly that no traces of his footsteps are left behind, and so gently that he does not trample human beings.

The Tengu, likewise a supernatural being, appears in two different forms: as raven-tengu with the beak of a bird, or else with a human face and an enormous nose resembling a sausage, the latter being a favorite subject for all kinds of peculiar or comical representations. The origin of this mythical creation seems to be the Persian-Grecian griffin. Half man, half eagle, he is the king of the feathered songsters.

The Japanese saga of the bird catcher who fries and devours the Tengu chickens as soon as they come out of the egg, and the saga of the hero Yoshitsume, who instructs the Tengu king in the art of fencing, are represented by innumerable carvers. It is also said that the natives of Funtan have human faces, but have wings and the beak of a bird.

The jugglers who travel through the villages with their monkeys, are a frequent subject for the Netsuke carver. The only native Japanese monkey has a short tail, is related to the Chinese tscheliensis, has a rose-red face, long, fine, grey or greyish-brown fur and red callous spots behind. He is very easy to train and is taken around by the monkey juggler. The wild as well as the juggler's monkey, clad in a jacket, is one of the favorite subjects for plastic art and painting (Plate XII). In Taoism and Buddhism the monkey plays a great part; in the former religion he is depicted holding a peach, the symbol of longevity.

The fox belongs to the class of animals who, according to Japanese belief, can transform themselves into human figures (Plate XV, 4). With all kinds of supernatural gifts, he unites desire and vexation.   At the age of fifty he can transfigure himself into a human being, at the age of one hundred into a beautiful girl, and when he has grown to be a thousand years old, he acquires nine tails and becomes a divinity.   As a Buddhist and Shintoist saga figure he is the creator of all sorts of undesired complications in human life, and in Shintoism he is the messenger of the rice god Ianri. There are seven such fox spirits among whom the crystal fox is the most dangerous rogue.

The lion (Plate III, 2), the king of the four-footed animals, the symbol of craft, has been introduced into Japan from China. In the East-Asiatic art he bears only a faint resemblance to the real lion.   He is adorned with beautiful locks of hair, amuses himself among peonies or plays with a ball, the holy trinket, a crystal cylinder which he either has rolling loosely in his mouth or holds under his right paw.   The entire representation resembles that of our conventional heraldic lion.

The tiger is (Plate III, 1), like the phoenix, the dragon and the tortoise, a supernatural animal, a symbol of craft, also the king of the mountain animals.   Like the other animals he was brought into Japan from India via China, in his conventional form. He resembles a striped cat, is supposed to become white at the age of five hundred, and live to be one thousand years. He is associated with bamboo.

The lemmings, although a plague in Japan, are an object of interest to young and old. Mice are very scarce. White and colored rats and mice are kept for amusement.

The hare and rabbit appear very often in the sagas of Japan in connection with the full moon and reach the age of 1000. The hare pounds mochi in a rice mortar in the moonlight. In Taoism he pounds the drugs to make the elixir of life. The head-cloth of the hare points to the heavy work he has to perform. He gives the Japanese workman a feeling of strength.

The Japanese horse, a kind of pony with short neck, bushy mane and heavy hair, is one of the first domestic animals. He has always been and still is used for riding and as carrier, but is never driven.

While the two-humped camel is present in South and Central Asia, the dromedary with one hump is found in West Asia only. A few living species may have found their way to Japan from time to time.

The only Japanese stag is smaller and more slender than ours and has light spots like a buck. Neither the goat, yagi, nor the lamb are indigenous to Japan. The steer in Japan is the symbol of the popular god of calligraphy who lived in the 9th century A. D.

The elephant, (Plate III, 3), has ever been symbolized as praying to Siva. In China he is symbolic of craft, a son of the dragon and a pig, and in Japan, where he is only known by the Chinese images, he is considered a great friend of children.

The wild boar is the only representative of the four-footed animals of Japan that resembles his European brother.

The cuckoo, comes at the end of the fifth month from fairy land, and with his calling warns the farmer to plant the rice. According to the East-Asiatic version, the cuckoo and the moon belong together like the lion and the peony, the tiger and bamboo, etc.

A tortoise, according to the Hindu legend, carries an elephant, who in turn carries the world. She belongs to the four Chinese supernatural

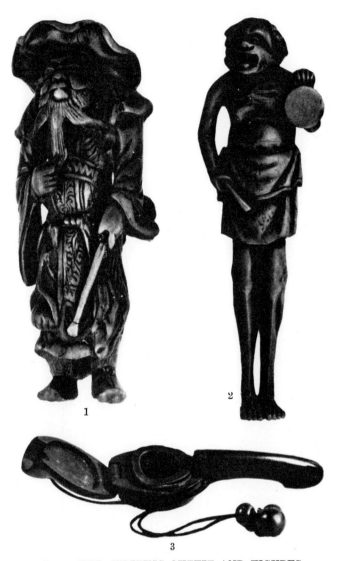

PLATE XVI—WRITING OUTFIT AND FIGURES

1. Dutchman (wood). 2. Man and drum, (wood). 3. Writing
outfit, (wood).

animals, is supposed to attain a fabulous age and then acquire a long-haired tail. She is a symbol of longevity. Her tail seems to be attached to the hind part of the back like a wreath of long green hair.

The cat, (Plate IV, 1), often with a short, mutilated tail, belongs also in Japan to the domestic animals. The dog is a domestic animal which is found everywhere in large numbers. A small pet-dog was first introduced from China by the Portuguese, in the 17th century named Chin "a hideous monstrosity, but an aristocrat, with two large, protruding rolling eyes and a tiny flat nose." The European dog was imported into Japan a relatively short time ago.

The octopus, or inkfish, were able, according to the legend, to draw down into the deep with their enormous arms an entire ship. Their round-shaped eyes and their nose which is shaped like a funnel give them a human appearance. In the East-Asiatic saga they play an important part, pursue beautiful maidens and make love to them under the water. The head with a long funnel nose reminds the Japanese of a Shiofuki mask. The octopus is caught by lowering an empty crock to the bottom of the sea into which he likes to crawl. On the other hand, the Japanese, in case of shipwreck, are said to tie a rope to the octopus and to let him down into the sea in order that he may find valuable earthen ware pots and bring them with him when he is drawn to the surface.

The snake is a symbol of retaliation, which is sometimes more fully illustrated, as for instance: a worm swallowed by a toad, a snake whirled around the toad, the snake attacked by a boar, the latter threatened by a hunter, the hunter pursued by a devil.

The Venus shell, is always mentioned in connection with passionate love and constancy. Very often the reproductions show the Venus shell as holding between its shells the foot of a Kappa, or the hip-cloth of a man. The bride, in order that she may prepare the wedding soup, is presented with a bowl of Venus shells.

The day before "Bon" the most ceremonious of all Buddhist festivities, the twelfth day of the seventh month, on the occasion of the funeral ceremony, the tombstones of the forefathers are placed upon a platform which is called the spirit altar, in order that their spirits may temporarily be among their own people. Above the altar is a rope to which, in addition to the millet and the lotus fruit, eggplants are fastened. The eggplant Netsuke is probably a reminder of such a ceremony.

The lotus flower, with its beautiful white blossoms, grows in slimy water, and for the devout Buddhists is an emblem of the human soul which, after having left the pleasures of this world, aspires to godly purity.

The frequent occurrence of Netsukes which represent, in a smaller form, the masks that are worn in No plays (Plate VI, VII), indicates perhaps that the finest works of art were made for the most intellectual people. For the old No play was a religious drama which, on account of its wonderfully descriptive and interlarded quotations from the Buddhist writings, and the quotations from Chinese poetry, could only be understood by the highly educated class of people. The anonymous librettists were, for the most part, Buddhist monks (14-16th century) while the authors of the well-known No plays (about 230 A. D.) composed only the music and the pantomime dances. During the entire Tokugawa period (1602-1868), the troups of actors were made up of noblemen, who acted ancient plays similar to our mystery and moral plays, and prized highly the old costumes and conventional masks, some of which dated from the eighth century and others from the religious temple dances performed in honor of the gods and called Kagura. Only those actors who took the part of females or supernatural beings wore masks. The diversity of the Japanese Netsuke masks is astounding. There are the beauty, the fox a special favorite, demons with horns and three eyes, a satyr with horns and the snout of a goat, Uzume, etc.

It is difficult to determine, by means of physiognomical analysis, the meaning of the face expression and the sort of human character which the carver originally intended to represent. Neither Darwin, nor any of the modern authors like Mantegazza, make such clear distinction in the facial expressions, which result from the various emotions: contentment, cheerfulness, joy, happiness, sensuousness, beatitude or on the other hand, displeasure, discouragement, grief, sorrow, pain, etc., as would permit a layman to classify and determine a certain mask when he has nothing else to be guided by except the emotions which are displayed in the features of the mask.

In regard to the artist names on these masks, I doubt whether in many cases they do not represent the name of the carver who originally created the mask life-size, instead of that of the Netsuke carver. While the masks, which represent men, show a particularly positive and strong expression, even in cases where they are not supposed to show any marked emotion, the masks of women, on the other hand, often appear without expression. The only sign of tragedy is the absence of the smile which the Japanese woman is always supposed to wear for the family and friends. She may cease to smile, but no spasm of pain or anxiety must appear on the fair face with its downcast eyes. The countenance must be unlined by the invisible harrow of thought, unstained by tears.

PARTIAL BIBLIOGRAPHY

PARTIAL BIBLIOGRAPHY

Anderson, W., A Handbook for travellers in Central and Northern Japan etc.

Baudoin, A. F. and A. J., Catalogue of Japanese Art objects (La Haye 1891).

Behrens, W. L., On certain traces of evolution noticed in Japanese art, Transactions and Proceedings of the Japan Society, vol. V, part 4, London, 1902.

Bing, S., Collection, Treasure of Japanese Figures, 3 years, Leipzig 1888-91.

Bowes, James Lord, Japanese marks and seals (3 parts, London 1882).

Brinckmann, Justus, Hamburg Museum for Art and Craft (Leipzig 1894).

Brinkley, F., Japan, Its History, Arts and Literature. 12 vols. J. B. Millet Co., Boston and Tokyo 1904 (T. C. and E. C. Jack, London and Edinburgh). Vol. VII.

Burty, Philippe, Collection of Japanese and Chinese art objects (Paris 1891).

Dollfus, Jean, Catalogue on Japanese Netsukes. By Adrien Dollfus with the collaboration of Messrs. P. Deshayes and S. Kawamoura. With 1 plate containing 7 illustrations (Paris, Dec. 1889).

Gilbertson, Edward, The art of collecting. I. Japanese Netsukes (in The Studio II. No. 10. January 1894, London).

Gilbertson, E., Selections from the descriptive catalogue of Netsukes and Japanese miscellanies in the Gilbertson Collection, with an introduction (Printed by Twiss & Son, 9 High Street, Ilfracombe 1889).

de Goncourt, Edmond, The house of an artist (new edition, 2 volumes, Paris 1881).

Goncourts, Catalogue of, Arts of the Far East (Paris 1897).

Gonse, Louis, Catalogue of the retrospective exhibition of Japanese Art (Paris 1883).

Gonse, Louis, The Japanese art (2 volumes, Paris 1883).

Griffis, William Elliot, Japanese ivory carvings (in Harper's Magazine, vol. 76, No. 455, April 1888).

Hart, Ernest, Lectures on Japanese art work. With a catalogue of the objects exhibited, and an index of Japanese artists etc. (Society for the encouragement of arts, manufactures, and commerce; London, printed by W. Trounce, 10 Gough Square, Fleet Street, E. C. 1887).

Hitomi, I., Japan, Essay on the customs and institutions, with 74 illustrations on separate plate (Paris 1900).

Huish, Marcus B., Catalogue of signatures of Japanese makers of lacquer, metal work, netsukes, etc. (Privately printed for the Fine Art Society, London 148 New Bond Street, 1888).

Huish, Marcus B., The evolution of a Netsuke (in "Transactions and Proceedings of the Japan Society," vol. III, part 4, London 1897).

Huish, Marcus B., Japan and its art (2nd ed., London 1892).

Humbert, A., Illustrated Japan (Paris 1870).

Lawrence, Sir Trevor, Bart. Catalogue of the collection of Japanese works of art. By Marcus B. Huish (Privately printed, London 1895).

Muller, F. W. K., Something on No-masks in "T'oung pao" (Leiden).

Regamey, Felix, Practical Japan (Paris 1897).

Titsingh, J., The Japanese Art Collection (Amsterdam 1893).

Tomkinson, Michael, A Japanese collection (2 volumes, London 1898).

Trower, H. Seymour, Netsukes, their makers, use and meaning (in "Magazine of arts," March 1889, London, Cassell & Co.).

Trower, H. Seymour, Netsukes and Okimonos (in "Japanese Treasure of Forms," collected by S. Bing, etc., 3 years, Leipzig 1888-91).